you can RENEW this item from
home by visiting our Website at
www.woodbridge.lioninc.org or by
calling (203) 389-3433

Life & Times in 20th-Century America

America

Volume 1: Becoming a Modern Nation

1900–1920

Greenwood Publishing Group

Library of Congress Cataloging-in-Publication Data
Life & times in 20th-century America / by Media Projects, Inc.
    p. cm
     Includes bibliographical references and indexes.
  Contents: v. 1. Becoming a modern nation, 1900-1920 — v. 2. Boom times, hard times,
1921-1940 — v. 3. Hot and cold wars, 1941-1960 — v. 4. Troubled times at home,
1961-1980 — v. 5. Promise and change, 1981-2000.
  ISBN 0–313–32570–7 (set: alk. paper)—ISBN 0–313–32571–5 (v. 1: alk. paper) —
ISBN 0–313–32572–3 (v. 2: alk. paper)—ISBN 0–313–32573–1 (v. 3: alk. paper) —
ISBN 0–313-32574–X (v. 4: alk. paper)—ISBN 0–313–32575–8 (v. 5: alk. paper)
  1. United States—History—20th century. 2. United States—Social conditions—20th
century. 3. United States—Social life and customs—20th century. I. Media Projects
Incorporated.
E741.L497 2004
973.91—dc21   2003044829

British Library Cataloguing in Publication Data is available.

Library of Congress Catalog Card Number: 2003044829
ISBN: 0–313–32570–7 (set)
    0–313–32571–5 (vol. 1)
    0–313–32572–3 (vol. 2)
    0–313–32573–1 (vol. 3)
    0–313–32574–X (vol. 4)
    0–313–32575–8 (vol. 5)

First published in 2004

Greenwood Press, 88 Post Road West, Westport, CT 06881
An imprint of Greenwood Publishing Group, Inc.
www.greenwood.com

Printed in the United States of America

The paper used in this book complies with the
Permanent Paper Standard issued by the National
Information Standards Organization (Z39.48–1984).

10 9 8 7 6 5 4 3 2 1

Media Projects, Inc.
Managing Editor: Carter Smith
Writer: Charles A. Wills
Editor: Carolyn Jackson
Production Editor: Jim Burmester
Indexer: Marilyn Flaig
Designer: Amy Henderson
Copy Editor: Elin Woodger

Contents

Life in a New Century

In 1900, most Americans were hopeful. Thirty-five years had passed since the end of the Civil War, and in that time the nation had grown and changed. In 1860, just before the war began, the country had fewer than 31 million people in thirty-three states. Most people lived east of the Mississippi River. Now there were almost 76 million people in forty-five states stretching over 3,000 miles to the Pacific Ocean. In 1906, Oklahoma would become a state, followed by Arizona and New Mexico in 1912. Their entrance to the union would create the pattern of states on the continent that we know today.

One reason for hope had to do with new advances. By 1900, the nation contained one-third of all the world's train tracks. Government and businesses were wired for electricity and telephones. Nearly 90 percent of Americans could read. More than 16 million students were in school. There were more students in the United States than in any other nation.

As Americans looked forward to the new century, they wondered how their country would keep changing. In 1899, future president Theodore Roosevelt stated that the 1900s meant new responsibilities for the United States. "The twentieth century looms before us with the fate of many nations," he said. "Let us therefore boldly...win the goal of true national greatness."

New Immigrants

One reason that the U.S. population had grown so quickly was new immigration, or people moving to the United States from other countries. Immigration had grown rapidly since the 1880s, when over 5 million new immigrants arrived. During the first decade of the 1900s, the number of new

CLOCKWISE: **The Wright brothers' plane lifts off; "Uncle Sam" seeks World War I recruits; women march for voting rights.** (All photos: Library of Congress)

immigrants rose to over 9 million. For six of the first fifteen years of the twentieth century, more than 1 million new immigrants arrived each year.

New immigrants did more than increase America's population. They also brought new languages and cultures to the United States. Most came from southern and eastern Europe, especially from the countries of Italy, Austria-Hungary, and Russia. The immigrants were often Jewish or Roman Catholic.

During the nineteenth century, Norwegian and German settlers had moved to rural or frontier areas of the United States. Early twentieth century immigrants settled in cities. They sometimes came into conflict with those who had settled there before them. The Irish had faced similar problems when they first arrived in American cities in the 1840s.

Still, the twentieth-century immigrants were grateful to leave behind difficult lives in their old countries. They willingly accepted new hardships here. Many worked in factories at low wages for long hours. They also lived in crowded tenements or large apartment buildings with unsafe conditions. Soon they began to take on American ways. This process of becoming part of a new culture is known as *assimilation*. Adults learned English at libraries and at community centers called settlement houses. Their children learned it at school. Immigrants adopted American foods and clothing. Those with long names often shortened them as part of becoming American. As one Eastern European immigrant in 1900 said of these old names, "Nothing good ever came to us

1900
Republican William McKinley is reelected president, defeating Democrat William Jennings Bryan.

1901
President McKinley is killed by an assassin. Vice President Theodore Roosevelt becomes the next president.

1902
The United Mine Workers leads a five-month strike involving 147,000 coal miners. The strike cripples the coal-mining industry. As winter approaches and the need for coal increases, President Theodore Roosevelt steps in to negotiate an end to the strike. Miners win a pay raise.

1902
Journalist Lincoln Steffens writes a series of articles about corruption in city government. The articles are then published together in a book called *The Shame of the Cities*.

European immigrants arrive at Ellis Island in New York in about 1905. (Library of Congress)

while we bore them; possibly we'll have more luck with the new names."

In cities like New York and Chicago, immigrants often found work and homes with the help of local politicians. Large political organizations, called machines because they worked predictably, attracted immigrants. In return, once they became citizens, many immigrants voted for a machine's candidates. Often the candidates were Irish and had arrived only a generation

1903

Produced by inventor Thomas Edison and directed by filmmaker Edwin S. Porter, the movie *The Great Train Robbery* is released. The twelve-minute-long movie is the first Western ever pro-duced. In addition to a train robbery, audi-ences also witness a horseback chase and a running gunfight.

1903

Ida Tarbell publishes *The History of Standard Oil Company*, which examines what she sees as the ruthless methods John D. Rockefeller used to build his oil company.

1903

Orville Wright successfully flies the first airplane at Kitty Hawk, North Carolina.

1906

A major earthquake strikes San Francisco, California, killing at least 500 people and destroying 28,000 buildings.

before. By 1920, more recent immigrants of Italian, Jewish, and Eastern European backgrounds had become politicians. Among them were New York's Fiorello La Guardia and Illinois's Anton Cermak.

As immigrants tried to work their way into American society, some native-born citizens harassed them with discriminatory laws and personal attacks. They regarded Catholics, Jews, and immigrants as "aliens" who should leave the United States. These beliefs led to the rebirth of a violent hate group known as the Ku Klux Klan in 1915. The original Ku Klux Klan had focused on attacking African Americans after the Civil War. The new version of the Klan targeted Jews and Catholics as well. For example, many historians believe that the Klan had a role in the lynching of Leo Frank, a Jewish Georgia businessman who was murdered in 1915.

The United States began to pass laws to slow immigration. Some Americans were concerned that if too many immigrants from places outside of Western Europe came to America, the country would change for the worse. In 1906, the San Francisco School Board voted to separate, or segregate, Japanese, Chinese, and Korean children from white children. When Japan's government complained, President Theodore Roosevelt made what became known as the "Gentleman's Agreement" in 1907 with Japan. He agreed to force San Francisco schools to allow Chinese, Japanese, and Korean students to attend classes with whites. In return, Japanese officials agreed not to allow any more Japanese and Korean immigration to the United States. (Japan ruled

1906

Upton Sinclair publishes his novel *The Jungle*. The novel describers the dangerous and filthy conditions of Chicago's meatpacking industry.

1907

Theater producer Florenz Ziegfeld creates "The Ziegfeld Follies," an annual show featuring female chorus lines and a steady stream of stars. The Follies would remain popular for the next several decades.

1907

An economic crisis known as the Panic of 1907 takes place. The crisis ends when bankers, led by New York millionaire J. P. Morgan, loan the government money.

1907

In what becomes known as the "Gentlemen's Agreement," the United States and Japan agree to limit the number of Japanese and Koreans allowed to immigrate to the United States.

Korea at the time, so it controlled immigration from Korea.)

In 1917, the U.S. Congress passed another immigration law. The new law required a literacy test for all potential new immigrants. Since most Asians did not read or speak English, this prevented many from staying in America. Immigration from Asia would be tightly controlled until 1965.

African American Rights

Racial segregation and conflict in the first two decades of the twentieth century did not only involve new immigrants. Some problems between the races had lingered since the Civil War. Beginning in the 1870s, laws mandating separation of the races were increasingly enforced in the South. This custom was bolstered by the 1896 Supreme Court decision *Plessy v. Ferguson*, which declared racial segregation to be legal. Lynching (hanging deaths carried out by mobs) rose rapidly during the early twentieth century. One thousand African Americans were lynched between 1900 and 1914 alone. Despite this violence and international campaigns against it by activists such as Ida B. Wells-Barnett, no federal law against lynching was passed. Mob violence and discrimination in the South was one reason why many African Americans sought new lives in the Northeast, Midwest, and West.

In 1914, war broke out in Europe. At the time, the war was known as the Great War. It would later be called World War I. In the war, Germany, Italy, and Austria-Hungary faced Great Britain, France, and Russia. In 1917,

1908

Explorers Robert Peary and Matthew Henson reach the North Pole.

Republican William Howard Taft wins the presidential election.

1909

The National Association for the Advancement of Colored People is founded.

1910

Heavyweight boxing champion Jack Johnson easily defeats former champion James J. Jeffries to keep his title.

1911

The United States Supreme Court orders that Standard Oil, which controls 90 percent of the oil-refining industry, be broken into smaller companies.

the United States entered the war on the side of Great Britain and its allies. While some African Americans would fight in segregated units in the war, many others moved north to find new work. They replaced soldiers who went to fight in Europe. Between 1914 and 1918, about 500,000 African Americans migrated north at the height of what would be called the Great Migration. Newly arriving blacks often found that the North was not free of racial prejudice. Mobs there and in the Midwest sometimes attacked African American workers. There were race riots in some cities, but most African Americans chose to stay in their new homes.

Country Life and City Life

In the early twentieth century, the United States was becoming an urban nation. Millions of new immigrants had dramatically increased the size of the United States' population. Almost all of the newcomers had settled in New York and other large cities. By 1900, only 32 percent of Americans worked in agriculture. This was a huge drop from 1776, when 90 percent of Americans were farmers.

While the percentage of Americans working as farmers fell, the actual number of farmers in America increased. By 1916, there were 6.4 million farms, which was a higher number than ever. These farms took up 879 million acres, twice as many acres as they did in 1860. With new machines, farmers were very productive. Corn, wheat, tobacco, cattle, and dairy prod-

1912
Democrat Woodrow Wilson defeats Republican Willian Howard Taft and Progressive Party candidate Theodore Roosevelt to become president.

1912
The luxury steamship *Titanic* hits an iceberg on its first voyage across the Atlantic Ocean. Because the ship carries too few lifeboats, more than 1,500 passengers drown.

1913
The federal goverment imposes income taxes for the first time.

1914
Mass-production techniques allow automaker Henry Ford to drop the price of a Model T Ford to $490. In 1908, when the car was first released, it had cost $850.

ucts were the main crops. Each region had its specialty. The need to feed large numbers of new immigrants and soldiers who would fight the Great War led to greater demand for farm products. The years 1900 to 1920 were to be a golden age for American farmers.

Meanwhile, city factories, offices, mines, and shops offered jobs to other Americans. This changed where people lived. By 1920, more people lived in areas of 2,500 or more inhabitants than in rural areas.

Most city dwellers lived in apartments. Poorer families lived in tenements, large connected buildings. Well-to-do families might choose the apartment-hotel, which had telephones, bathrooms, and maid service. Middle-class families usually lived in three- to four-room apartments, with fewer conveniences. They chose large buildings near streetcar lines. Others lived in one-room apartments called efficiencies and prepared their food in

Rural vs. Urban Population

Source: U.S. Census

1917

In April, the United States declares war on Germany and enters World War I. The war will last until November 1918. During the war, total U.S. deaths will reach about 116,000. More than half of those deaths will come from the worldwide spread of influenza.

1918

President Woodrow Wilson pushes for the formation of the League of Nations by issuing a proposal called the Fourteen Points. The proposal's goal is to create permanent peace.

1919

The United States Congress approves voting rights for women by passing the Nineteenth Amendment to the Constitution.

1920

Republican Warren G. Harding wins the presidential election.

tiny kitchens called kitchenettes. Many city dwellers lived as boarders, or paid guests, or took them in. In 1910, one-third to one-half of all city residents were boarders.

In the early twentieth century, up to 10 percent of a city's residents slept in flophouses, or very inexpensive rooming houses where single rooms could be rented. By 1890, photographer Jacob Riis had begun documenting lives in these areas of New York City. That year, he published many of his photos in *How the Other Half Lives*. This book spurred reform in city living conditions.

Outside of cities, a new kind of neighborhood, called the suburb, became more common in the early 1900s. The suburb was separate from the city but near it, and it had more open space. In the late nineteenth century, only rich people could afford to live in the suburbs. Lack of public transportation made traveling back and forth between city and suburb too expensive for most people. But in the twentieth century, cities developed streetcar lines and trains that rode out to the suburbs, so working people began moving to them. Some new suburbs, like Blue Island, Illinois, were even developed for blue-collar workers.

An Assassination and a New President

By 1900, the U.S. economy was booming, thanks in part to the discovery of gold in Alaska in 1896. In addition, the United States was expanding its territory. In the Spanish-American War of 1898, the United States had defeated Spain to win the Philippines, Guam, and Puerto Rico. It made Hawaii a U.S. territory in 1898.

The assassination of President McKinley
(Library of Congress)

The 1900 election repeated the contest of 1896 between William Jennings Bryan on the Democratic ticket and President William McKinley on the Republican. Bryan, a spellbinding public speaker, wanted to expand the nation's money supply by making silver the standard that guaranteed the money's worth. But McKinley easily won reelection. To replace his vice president who had died in office, McKinley chose a rich, young Spanish-American War hero: Governor Theodore Roosevelt of New York.

On September 6, 1901, at the Pan-American Exposition in Buffalo, New York, a Polish anarchist named Leon Czolgosz shot President McKinley. (An anarchist is someone who rebels against all government and believes it should be abolished.) Eight days later, McKinley died, and Theodore Roosevelt became president. He was 42, the youngest man ever to hold the office.

Roosevelt was a new kind of president. He was energetic. He also had six playful children, who ranged in age from four to seventeen. They brought new life to a presidential mansion usually filled with older politicians. The young children played morning games with the president. The older boys hit baseballs on the lawn. The eldest girl, Alice, was athletic, brash, and fashionable. Her best-known outfit was her "Alice blue gown." To make room for the president's large family, his staff was moved to what is now known as the West Wing. Roosevelt made official the name given the executive residence when it was remodeled after the War of 1812: the White House.

President Roosevelt's wife, Edith, also added her style and elegance to the presidency. She supervised the modernization of the presidential mansion and helped to coordinate the many social events held there. Guests at the White House included the leading thinkers and artists of the time.

An Age of Reform

President Roosevelt often called the presidency a "bully pulpit." (Bully was a slang word in those days for marvelous or excellent, and a pulpit is a place where sermons are preached.) Roosevelt tried to use his high office to improve the lives of people from all walks of life. Roosevelt's reforms were part of what became known as the Progressive Movement. Progressives believed the government had a role to play in encouraging human progress. Like William Jennings Bryan had, Roosevelt believed that wealthy bankers and industrialists in the Northeast and around the Great Lakes held too much power. But unlike Bryan's family, Roosevelt's family was a part of that establishment. His father had been a wealthy New York merchant and director on many corporate boards. Teddy, as the president was called, tried to make his reforms moderate. Still, he angered people in the Republican Party who opposed even small changes. Roosevelt thought that progress required change. In his autobiography, written in 1913, after he had left the presidency, he wrote this about those who opposed change:

"I have always maintained that our worst revolutionaries today are those... who do not see and will not admit that there is any need for change. ... If these [people] had lived at an earlier time in our history, they would have ... opposed free speech and free assembly, and voted against free schools; they are the men who to-day oppose minimum wage laws, insurance of workmen against the ills of industrial life and the reform of our legislators and our courts, which can alone render such measures possible. ... It is these reactionaries ... who, by 'standing pat' on industrial injustice, incite ... industrial revolt, and it is only we who advocate political and industrial democracy who render possible the progress of our American industry ... with a minimum of friction [and] with a maximum of justice."

Theodore Roosevelt (1858–1919) (AT LEFT), **the twenty-sixth President of the United States, with the Scottish-born American conservationist John Muir (1838–1914) on Glacier Point in Yosemite, California.** (Library of Congress)

Roosevelt was not alone in his beliefs. Many groups were working for causes that they thought would improve the country. Some people wanted to forbid the sale of alcohol. Others wanted to improve working conditions for laborers and get rid of slum housing. Still others wanted to allow women the right to vote. Ongoing was a fight for rights for immigrants and African Americans, although none of the presidents of this period embraced that fight. This mix of social action made the early twentieth century a time of reform. It would be known as the Progressive Era.

During the first of his two full terms, Roosevelt focused on two causes: trust-busting and conservation of natural resources. Since the 1890s, Roosevelt had argued that a few owners controlled all major businesses through legal arrangements called trusts. He thought this building of trusts showed the excess greed of the rich. To him, trusts were dangerous because they could lead to social division and revolution. Yet Roosevelt did not want to destroy all trusts; he only wanted to break up the most powerful.

In one of many efforts, President Roosevelt and the Justice Department brought suit under a law called the Sherman Anti-Trust Act (1890) against the merger of several transcontinental railroads into a "holding company" called Northern Securities Company. (Holding companies are individual companies that own parts or all of other companies in order to control them.) In 1903, the government won its case in court against Northern Securities Company. The U.S. Supreme Court later upheld the victory.

Roosevelt was also an outdoorsman who believed in an active, strenuous life. He was alarmed at how quickly developers and settlers were cutting into the nation's national resources. He publicly criticized what he called "the man who skins the land."

To promote interest in conservation, he spoke to the public and fought for the passage of new laws. Among his greatest accomplishments was the expansion of the forest reserves. In 1905, he pushed the Congress to create the United States Forest Service. In doing so, he helped preserve almost 200 million acres of government land from development, mostly in the Northwest and Alaska.

During the early twentieth century, children like this young girl often worked long hours in factories. (Library of Congress)

Muckrakers and Labor Unions

Between 1900 and 1910, reporters called "muckrakers" helped to uncover corruption in government and business. The term *muckraker* came from President Roosevelt, who thought reporters' views of the nation's problems was too negative. (He took it from *The Pilgrim's Progress* by English writer John Bunyan, who said muckrakers always looked down into the muck, or mud.)

Soon the term *muckraker* took on new meanings. In *McClure's* magazine, Ida Tarbell attacked the Standard Oil trust, and Lincoln Steffens called for reform in the cities. Upton Sinclair's novel *The Jungle* showed filth and corruption in the meatpacking industry. Muckrakers built support for legislation such as the Meat Inspection Act and the Pure Food and Drug Act of 1906. They also helped speed the breakup of the Standard Oil Company in 1911.

As the nation industrialized, conditions in its mines and factories were dreadful. Workers—some of them children—toiled long hours for miserable wages. Both the machinery and the workplace were often dangerous. In 1904, for example, 27,000 workers were killed on the job. In New York City alone, 50,000 accidents were reported.

Unions organized to take the part of workers against big business. Often they were ignored. Usually, government took the side of owners. In the early twentieth century, the American Federation of Labor was the nation's largest union. Its ranks included 80 percent of all union members; all were skilled white men. Other unions included the International Ladies Garment Workers Union and the Industrial Workers of the World. Miners organized under the United Mineworkers Union struck Pennsylvania coal companies in 1902. They wanted higher wages, shorter hours, and recognition of their union. Responding to public pressure over the price of coal, President Roosevelt persuaded the owners to negotiate. The miners returned to work.

Still, most workplaces remained unsafe. It took a single event to finally convince most people that factory reforms were needed. On March 25, 1911, a small fire started in a rag bin at the Triangle Shirtwaist Company in New York City. The fire soon covered the clothing factory floor. Within an hour, 146 workers, mostly young immigrant women from Italy and Eastern Europe, choked to death from smoke inhalation. They could not escape, because owners kept the doors locked or blocked. With no other way out, some jumped out windows, falling ten stories to their death. After the fire, New York and other states passed factory safety laws.

Prohibition and Moral Reform

Carrie Nation
(Library of Congress)

Between 1900 and 1920, many groups worked for prohibition, or an end to the production and sale of alcohol. Even before the turn of the century, some Protestant groups and other moral leaders fought to ban alcohol. One leader, Carrie Nation, became famous for attacking saloons with her ax. She and other prohibition supporters fought the sale of alcohol because they believed that "demon rum" led families to break up and drinkers to fall into ruin.

But alcohol was hard to ban. In many countries from which immigrants came, saloons were widely accepted as social centers. This made some U.S.-born community leaders worried that foreign-born people might plan revolution in saloons. After a foreigner killed President McKinley, these fears increased. One side benefit of prohibition, some reasoned, would be to cut down on the places that immigrants could gather.

In 1919, Congress passed the Volstead Act. It enforced the Eighteenth Amendment to the Constitution, which prohibited the sale and transportation of alcohol. For the next twelve years, it would be illegal for Americans to make, buy, or sell liquor.

Women Get the Vote

Feminists are people who believe that women should have the same social, economic, and political rights as men. Since the late nineteenth century, feminist leaders such as Elizabeth Cady Stanton and Susan B. Anthony had worked for women's rights. As the twentieth century began, feminists made progress toward their goals.

In many ways, women had become more active in society. Between 1900 and 1910, the number of women in the workplace had reached their largest numbers to that date, from 23.5 to 28.1 percent. Women had become the majority of teachers and made up substantial minorities of secretaries, telephone operators, and nurses. Socially, women became more open in talking about world affairs and racy subjects like sex. Some were even seen smoking in public.

In 1910, a new, stronger, movement to win women suffrage, or the right to vote, gained steam. By that time, four western states allowed women to vote. After years of lobbying Congress and the public, suffragists, as advocates of women's voting rights were called, found the support they needed. It came about largely as a result of some suffragists' support for the Great War. They made speeches and appeared at "Liberty Loan" rallies, which raised money for the war effort. "We have made women partners in the war," said President Woodrow Wilson.

In 1918, the House of Representatives approved a constitutional amendment to grant women the vote. The amendment failed to pass in the Senate in 1918. But in 1919, after three senators who did not support suffrage were not reelected, the House and Senate passed the amendment. It was ratified by three-quarters of the states in 1920. Women across America voted for the first time in November 1920.

That's Entertainment!

Charlie Chaplin
(Library of Congress)

As the U.S. population grew more diverse, so did entertainment. Boxing and baseball were the most popular spectator sports early in the century. Horse racing, which had always been popular in the South, moved north too. The best-known boxer was Jack Johnson, an African American who became heavyweight champion in 1908. So great was the racial prejudice against him that promoters immediately began looking for any white boxer—a "Great White Hope"—to defeat him. Johnson was taunted by racist white fans, but he was a hero among blacks and others. He retained the title of heavyweight champion until 1915.

In 1901, a second professional base-

Jack Johnson, heavyweight champion
(Library of Congress)

ball league, the American League, joined the National League, formed in 1876. The first World Series between the winning team in each league was played in 1903. Outstanding players of this era included the American League's Ty (Tyrus) Cobb, known for his nasty temper and aggressive style of play; and the National League's (John) Honus Wagner, who was as gentle and principled as Cobb was tough. In 1919, members of the Chicago White Sox were found to have purposely lost the World Series in exchange for money from gamblers. Baseball was so popular that even the so-called "Black Sox scandal" did not dim its appeal as the "national pastime."

Ty Cobb (LEFT) and "Shoeless Joe" Jackson (RIGHT), two of the greatest hitters in baseball history. In 1919, Jackson became involved in the "Black Sox" scandal, when he and seven other teammates on the Chicago White Sox took money from gamblers to lose the World Series. (Library of Congress)

In the early 1900s, almost every town had an "opera house," but operas were rarely performed there. Instead there might be a number of skits, musical and acrobatic acts, and comedians. Vaudeville, a combination of short acts by traveling performers, had begun after the Civil War. It would continue throughout the 1920s.

Now vaudeville had competition. Silent, moving pictures, or movies, had just been invented. In 1905, the first "nickelodeon," where people watched these movies, opened in Pittsburgh. It showed short films to people who paid a five-cent admission. Eight thousand nickelodeons opened over the next six years. They showed silent films, mostly about everyday life, to 25 million people a week. The main audiences were immigrants and laborers who did not speak English. The lack of an English soundtrack was no problem to them.

Soon movie companies were making full-length feature films. Major companies invented the idea of "movie stars" to attract regular viewers. The first stars were Charlie Chaplin, whose Little Tramp character debuted in 1914; and Mary Pickford, whose golden ringlets and sweet portrayals made her "America's Sweetheart." Although films were still silent, they were now socially acceptable for the opera house and the "movie palace."

Anyone wanting to know the day's events read a newspaper. In the early twentieth century, there were over 2,200 daily newspapers. About 15 million city dwellers bought a paper every day. Readers could get sports scores, laugh at the comics, and perhaps read an advice column. Although the first AM radio station was built in 1902, commercial broadcasts would not begin until 1920.

Popular fiction and magazines were aimed at the middle class, who could buy the advertised products. As more homes gained electricity, it was easier to read at night. The *Saturday Evening Post* was popular during this period. Many well-known writers contributed articles and short stories, and there were cartoons. Readers looking for adventure read books by Jack London. His novels, such as *Call of the Wild* and *White Fang*, were very popular. Girls and boys read series of books about Nancy Drew and the Hardy Boys, which had just begun publication.

Technological Advances

The inventions and advances of the early twentieth century matched or surpassed those in the late nineteenth century.

The greatest refinement of a nineteenth-century invention was the automobile. Early in the new century, automaker Henry Ford developed the assemblyline for production of cars. This increased the number of cars produced and lowered their cost. The introduction of the Model T Ford in 1908 put automobiles in reach of ordinary people, not just the wealthy. By 1915, there were about 2 million cars registered in the United States. By 1920, there were about 8 million. Tens of thousands of people worked in the auto industry. The automobile spurred the building of new highways and new businesses such as gas stations and repair shops.

Automaker Henry Ford
(Library of Congress)

Another invention was the radio, or wireless telegraph. The first radio transmission was sent across the Atlantic Ocean in 1901. At first, the radio had little effect on people's lives, but with advertising, a way was found to pay for its everyday use. The first commercial radio station, KDKA in Pittsburgh, Pennsylvania, began broadcasting in 1920.

Transportation changed forever with the airplane. Brothers Orville and Wilbur Wright designed a plane that Orville flew over Kitty Hawk, North Carolina, in December 1903. The plane flew for only twelve seconds on the first attempt. By 1905, the Wright brothers could keep a plane in the air for half an hour. The War Department contracted with them to produce the first army airplanes in 1909. Both Americans and Germans flew warplanes during World War I, but passenger air travel did not begin until the 1920s.

The United States engineered the building of the Panama Canal. The forty-mile waterway was built over several years on land leased from the Central American country of Panama. Called the "Path Between the Seas," the canal linked the Atlantic and Pacific Oceans. Ships no longer had to sail around the tip of South America on the way from the East Coast of North America to the West. The canal opened in 1914.

Politics after Theodore Roosevelt

Theodore Roosevelt was reelected by a landslide in 1904 but announced he would not run in 1908. Instead he helped Republican William Howard Taft defeat William Jennings Bryan, who ran a third time. As president, Taft followed some of Roosevelt's progressive thinking. During

William Howard Taft
(Private collection)

his term, Taft passed more antitrust laws than Roosevelt. A constitutional amendment to create an income tax also passed during his term.

Nonetheless, Roosevelt argued that Taft had not done enough to improve the lives of working people. Therefore, for the 1912 presidential election, Roosevelt decided he wanted to run again. When Taft won the Republican nomination, Roosevelt created the new Progressive Party. People called it the Bull Moose Party, because Roosevelt often boasted that he was as strong as a bull moose. Taft and Roosevelt split the Republican vote, and Democrat Woodrow Wilson was elected.

At this point, Wilson and the Democrats took over the progressive tradition. They implemented the new income tax and reformed the banking system. They also lowered tariffs, which were taxes against goods coming into the country that stifled foreign trade. President Wilson worked to keep the country out of the war that broke out in Europe in 1914. Austria-Hungary and Germany (later joined by Turkey and Bulgaria), the Central powers, opposed the Allied powers of England, France, Russia, and Serbia. By 1915, the Allied side also included Japan, Canada, Australia, New Zealand, South Africa, Italy, and Romania.

Into the Great War

The Great War was triggered by the assassination of Austro-Hungarian Archduke Franz Ferdinand by a gunman from Serbia. The underlying cause of the war was that the European powers had heavily armed themselves and were joined in secret pacts. An attack on one meant the others would join in. (After World War II, the Great War would be referred to as World War I.)

At first the United States was sympathetic toward the Allies but did not get involved in fighting. Even in 1915, after 128 Americans were killed when Germans sank the British passenger liner *Lusitania*, the United States did not join in. But in early 1917, Germany sank both Allied and American ships and killed more Americans. In March, President Wilson authorized naval attacks against German submarines. In a speech to Congress on April 2, 1917, he prepared the country for war, saying, "The world must be made safe for democracy." Four days later, both houses of Congress had declared war.

The United States readied for battle quickly; about 2 million men enlisted. The Draft Act became law on May 18, making enlistment in the military mandatory for all qualified men. By the end of the war, 24 million men, almost half of all American males, had registered. More than 2.7 million of them served in the army.

On the home front, the War Industries Board managed civilian businesses. It led carmakers and coal and oil producers to switch to war production. The Food and Fuel Administrations rationed fuel, so that people traveled less. To make more food available for the troops, citizens were asked to grow vegetable gardens and eat no meat on "Meatless Mondays."

American soldiers advance on German trenches in 1918. (National Archives)

Celebrities sold Liberty Bonds, or interest-bearing documents issued by the federal government to finance the war. Advertisers created ads to support the war and promote enlistment. One of the most successful recruitment posters was by James Montgomery Flagg. It showed Uncle Sam pointing his finger and saying, "I Want YOU for U.S. Army."

Broadway producer George M. Cohan quickly contributed a rousing patriotic song, "Over There." This became the unofficial marching song of U.S. troops. Composer Irving Berlin, a Russian immigrant, wrote the still-popular "God Bless America" for a patriotic show he created after he joined the army.

In June 1918, freshly trained U.S. troops under General John Pershing joined Allied forces in France, the center of fighting. U.S. troops took a large part in the Allied recapture of Belleau Wood, and in battles at St. Mihiel and the Meuse-Argonne forest. American heroes included Army Sergeant Alvin York, who captured 132 prisoners. York was a former conscientious objector, someone who argues he or she cannot serve in the military for reasons of conscience. Another hero was Army Air Corps Captain Eddie Rickenbacker, who shot down twenty-six German aircraft. U.S. troops were scheduled to be a major part of the invasion of Germany in 1919. But that invasion was unnecessary. In November 1918, the Germans signed an armistice, or peace treaty. The Great War was over.

Pilot Eddie Rickenbacker was a World War I hero. (Library of Congress)

About 112,000 U.S. soldiers died during the conflict. The war cost the United States $24 billion, plus another $11 billion in loans that the nation had to borrow from banks and other lenders. This increased the national debt from $1 billion in 1915 to $20 billion in 1920.

The Fourteen Points

In January 1918, six months before the war ended, President Wilson spoke to Congress about a postwar peace plan. He called it the Fourteen Points. One "point" called for "open covenants," not the secret alliances that European nations had had before the war era. Another said there should be free trade and open sea travel. Wilson's ideal plan rejected revenge against Germany. It also called for an "association of nations" to promote world peace.

Britain and France agreed to the world association, but the treaty they created would make peace difficult. The Treaty of Versailles, signed in 1919 at Versailles, France, called for Germany to pay them back for the costs of the war. The payments were called reparations.

Back in the United States, the Senate still had to ratify, or approve, the treaty. Certain powerful senators, called isolationists, opposed U.S. involvement in international affairs. They demanded that the proposed association of nations, now called the League of Nations, be removed from the treaty. But Wilson refused to return to Europe and try to negotiate a new treaty. Hurt by the rejection of senators in his own country, he went on a U.S. speaking tour to promote the league and overcome their opposition. On October 2, 1919, the president suffered a massive stroke that left him partly paralyzed. While he recuperated, Wilson made most of the important decisions. His wife, Edith, took care of the details of government.

The U.S. Senate did not ratify the Treaty of Versailles. Nevertheless, it went into effect, calling for terrible burdens on Germany and for a League of Nations. Because the United States refused to join the league, it stood no chance of success. In twenty years, Europe would plunge the world into war again.

Into the "Normal" 1920s

Theodore Roosevelt died in his sleep early in 1919. Wilson was too sick to run for reelection. Two of the era's major progressive voices were silenced. By 1920, there was other evidence that the Age of Reform was ending. One was a campaign of fear that communist radicals were about to take over the government. It was called the "Red Scare" because red was the symbol of communism.

In 1917, revolutionaries had overturned Czar Nicholas II of Russia and brought communist rule to that country. Some Americans were concerned that communists might take over the United States. The government began to monitor and deport people whom it considered radicals prone to violent overthrow. Between 1919 and 1920, the U.S. government under Attorney General Mitchell A. Palmer deported hundreds of radicals, including anarchist Emma Goldman. Future FBI Director J. Edgar Hoover, already working for the Department of Justice, called this Russian immigrant and fiery speaker America's most dangerous woman because of her ability to excite crowds.

In the presidential election of 1920, the Republicans nominated plain-spoken, Ohio-born Warren G. Harding for president, and Vermonter Calvin Coolidge for vice president. They called for "normalcy; not revolution," breaking away from the past two decades of reform. Their Democratic opponents, former Ohio governor James Cox for president and a distant cousin of Theodore Roosevelt's named Franklin D. Roosevelt for vice president, favored progressive government.

In November, Harding and Coolidge won in a landslide. Most of the 106 million Americans were tired of war abroad and change at home. They wanted normalcy. Soon the nation would enter into the Roaring Twenties, when every idea of normal changed again.

Chapter One

Family Life

A young African American mother (LEFT) bathes her child. President Theodore Roosevelt (RIGHT) brought his lively young family with him to the White House.
(Library of Congress)

Family life underwent great change in the beginning of the twentieth century. Many families moved from farms in the country to apartments in the city. Homes and apartments were more comfortable with the advent of indoor plumbing and electricity. Women had fewer children, but giving birth was safer. More children went to school rather than worked, and childhood was extended by the recognition of adolescence.

Americans experienced all these changes differently, depending upon their location and their social class.

At Home in City and Country

American families in this period were on the move. Immigrants moved thousands of miles to a new continent. Farmers moved to the city. City dwellers moved to the suburbs. Southern African American families moved north. Easterners moved west. A few Midwestern homeowners put their houses on planks and wheels and took them to another location. In New York City, nearly one-third of the 200,000 residents moved when their annual leases ended in May.

The automobile, of course, was the new prime mover of people. Cars were quickly becoming an essential family purchase. They were especially popular in suburbs and the countryside. In cities, public transportation also improved. New York City's first subway, the Interborough Rapid Transit (IRT), began operation in 1903. For a nickel, people could speed below horse and carriage, manure-clogged city streets to a destination miles away.

Between 1900 and 1920, the United States became a nation of city dwellers. In 1900, 48.5 million of the nation's 76 million people—more than six out of every ten Americans—lived in the country. By 1910, less than half of the nation's 92 million people lived there.

Farm families lived in simple houses. Sometimes there was a porch or another room added after the house was built. Nearly all farm families used an outhouse for a bathroom; indoor plumbing was not common until many years later. Heat was likely to come from a potbellied stove. Water for family use came from pumps attached to outside wells. Almost all newly manufactured furnishings came from a mail-order catalog. Farm families bought fewer things than families in cities. They spent much of their money on farm equipment, such as new tractors with internal combustion engines (like cars) and combines to harvest grain.

Farm families had plenty of money during the Great War (World War I, 1914–1918). When demand for food to feed the troops dropped at the war's end, farm prices plummeted. Family members had to look for other sources of income. Women took in laundry. Some husbands traveled out of state to look for seasonal work. Wives and children stayed behind to run the farm. Many farm families gave up farming and moved into the city.

Urban Ills

In cities, working-class and immigrant families made up much of the population. Their lives were a constant struggle to keep afloat financially and physically. Jobs were scarce, and the pay was low. Workplaces were more dangerous than farms. At home, crowding, lack of sanitation, and poor diet increased deaths, especially among children. In one Pennsylvania mining district, one in three children died before they were a year old. Novelist Upton Sinclair illustrated such tragedies in his book *The Jungle*, in which he reports how a child died after falling into contaminated waters under a wooden sidewalk.

The usual working-class apartment was small, poorly lit, and stuffy due to poor ventilation. Typically there were two bedrooms

A family of recent immigrants to New York in their New York tenement. (Museum of the City of New York)

A piano graces the living room of this middle-class New York apartment belonging to a Mrs. Elliott. (Museum of the City of New York)

The formal living room of the Vanderbilt family mansion on New York's "Millionaire's Row." (Museum of the City of New York)

and a kitchen. In the kitchen, a coal stove was used for cooking meals and heating the apartment. Bedrooms were cold at night. People often heated ceramic or stone bricks on the stove and took them to bed. Lighting was provided by kerosene lamps that had to be filled regularly, because working-class apartments would not get electricity, central heat, or gas for many years to come. The family got its water for cooking, bathing, and washing clothes from pumps in a hall sink that it shared with other families. Toilets were shared as well.

The typical middle-class apartment or house was larger with more modern conveniences. Many houses (and fewer apartments) had running water inside. Gas lamps lit most homes, but electricity was becoming a more common source of power. By 1920, more than a third of residences were wired for electricity. The vacuum cleaner was quickly becoming the era's most successful consumer invention, replacing sweeping by hand or beating rugs. By that time, central heating, delivered by "steam heat" through an iron radiator, was common. Fireplaces were no longer a source of heat but a center for family gatherings.

During this period, kitchens were redesigned so that workspaces were more convenient. Countertops alongside the sink made food preparation easier. Stoves were nearby, cupboards overhead. These new kitchens were called "servantless," although middle-class housewives usually had one helper in the kitchen.

Well-to-do families lived in apartment-hotels or in mansions of many rooms. (Some of the wealthiest Americans, such as the family of shipping king Cornelius Vanderbilt, not only kept a mansion on a section of New York's Fifth Avenue called "Millionaire's Row" but also had a second mansion in seaside resorts, such as Newport, Rhode Island.) They were cared for by servants, referred to as "domestic help," who came in daily or lived with them. Children's rooms were set apart, often on an upper floor. They slept, played, and ate most of their meals away from their parents, supervised by a nanny. The mother and father visited daily, for a limited time. Wives and husbands often had separate bedrooms.

The wealthy entertained more often than the middle class, usually in a fancy parlor. Dining rooms were large enough to host a crowd, and there were extra rooms for entertaining, such as ballrooms. Kitchens in mansions were in the basement. Outside were many gardens and a lawn where people might play croquet.

Modern Conveniences

During this period, more people began to eat food that could be quickly prepared. Although *The Settlement Cookbook* advised that cooking was "the way to a man's heart," fewer women cooked from scratch. By 1910, 70 percent of women baked bread at home, down 10 percent from twenty years earlier. By 1920, most Americans had some packaged food—such as pancake flour or Jello-O—in their diets.

Restaurants serving premade meals were introduced in cities. In Philadelphia and New York City, the Horn & Hardart Automat offered slices of meat loaf or pie in gleaming glass and metal compartments. Patrons bought a serving by putting a nickel in a slot. They then sat at cafeteria-style tables to eat.

An early advertisement for Jell-O. (Library of Congress)

Americans also became more aware of nutrition. Improved transportation allowed regular supplies of seasonal foods. Exotic fruits like strawberries, oranges, and pineapples were available for the first time. Food reformers, Drs. John and William Kellogg, challenged morning eating habits. They suggested that ready-made, packaged cereals like cornflakes and shredded wheat were healthier and more easily digested than eggs and bacon.

The Kellogg brothers introduced breakfast cereals in the early twentieth century as a healthy alternative to what were then more traditional American breakfasts of bacon and eggs. (New York Public Library Picture Collection)

At the start of the new century, modern hospitals were opening, but family doctors often made "house calls," visiting patients at their homes rather than treating them in their offices. For minor aches and illnesses, however, a doctor's visit was not always needed. By the early twentieth century, families also used more over-the-counter medications. They bought health aids such as aspirin and other nonprescription medicines. Many medicines for "female complaint" or "brain fatigue" contained liquor or opium, but manufacturers were not required to label them.

People also became more interested in personal hygiene. Now that many families had running water at home, they could bathe more frequently. Encouraged by advertising, they bought new personal products. Deodorants fought the ailment of body odor, and mouthwash cured "halitosis" (bad breath). Men began to shave with "safety razors," invented in 1901 by King C. Gillette. Safety razors featured a small, disposable blade and were less likely to cut the skin than the old straight-edge razor. Even so, not all of today's hygiene products were available. For example, shampoo was not available in stores until the 1920s. Before that time, people used bars of soap to wash their hair.

Childbirth and Mortality

Changes in health care in the early twentieth century also changed the way that expectant mothers went through pregnancy and childbirth.

In the middle and late nineteenth century, most women who gave birth in a hospital were poor. Large hospitals, which were often funded by local governments, were built to care for those who could not afford private care. Middle-class and wealthy families received routine "house call" visits from the family doctor. Usually, women from these families also gave birth at home, with the aid of a midwife. Most poor women could not afford to pay a midwife. Others had no separate room for the birth or lacked running water. Still others were not married and wanted to keep the birth a secret. Having a child "out of wedlock [marriage]" brought shame to both mother and child.

Early in the twentieth century, the new medical specialty of obstetrics was developed to deal with pregnancy and childbirth. A majority of white women began to have their babies delivered by doctors, not midwives. At first, doctors delivered babies at home. Later women came to hospitals. There they could receive anesthetics to put them to sleep and reduce their pain. Additionally, only in a hospital could doctors deliver babies surgically, by Caesarian section, if the delivery proved difficult. Mothers and newborns were safer.

Despite these advances, one woman died in every 154 births in 1910. Giving birth and the months just afterward were the most dangerous time of a woman's life. It was even more dangerous for babies. Ten percent of all infants—and 20 percent of African American infants—died before their first birthday. Many of them caught diseases and infections for which there was no cure.

Margaret Sanger, a visiting nurse in New York, became concerned about the effect of frequent pregnancy on the health of poor women. In 1914, she introduced the term *birth control* in her newspaper, *The Woman Rebel*. In 1916, Sanger opened a birth control clinic in Brooklyn. Ten days later, she was arrested for distributing obscene materials and sent to a workhouse (a prison for those convicted of minor offenses and put to work) for thirty days.

Many people viewed birth control as immoral, since they believed that it encouraged having sex outside of marriage for reasons other than having children. Sanger continued her work despite this opposition.

M-O-T-H-E-R

In 1914, Mother's Day was created as a national holiday. The next year, "M-O-T-H-E-R (The Word that Means the World to Me)" was a popular hit song. The words to that song, written by Howard Johnson, are written below.

M is for the million things she gave me,
O means only that she's growing old,
T is for the tears she shed to save me,
H is for her heart of purest gold;
E is for her eyes, with love-light shining,
R means right, and right she'll always be,
Put them all together, they spell "MOTHER,"
A word that means the world to me.

(Courtesy of ParlorSongs)

Babyhood and Childhood

Before 1900, a baby was typically breastfed for its first year. Now using cows' milk in bottles for feeding babies gained popularity. Experts praised bottle feeding for its cleanliness and efficiency. However, that cleanliness depended on sterilizing the bottle and pasteurizing the milk to reduce bacteria in it.

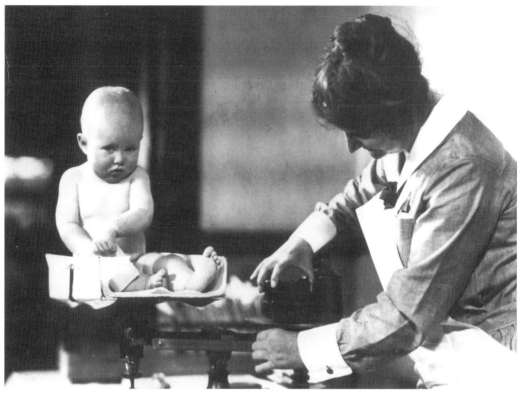

Hospital care for infants became more common for all Americans after the turn of the twentieth century. In this photograph, a nurse at the Mayo Clinic in Rochester, Minnesota, weighs a baby.
(Minnesota Historical Society)

Nevertheless, bottles made it easier for someone other than the mother to feed a baby. In the 1910s, an average of 2 million baby bottles were sold annually.

Once a baby left the hospital, another new medical specialist, the pediatrician, took over. By 1920, children paid an average of two visits a year to a pediatrician. During those visits, they would receive vaccinations, or doses of medicine aimed at preventing disease. (See Chapter 7, Health, Science, and Technology.)

In addition to the physical sciences like medicine, chemistry, and physics, psychiatrists, psychologists, and sociologists were beginning to lay down principles that they believed governed human development. The family was the focus of much of this "social science," and the mother was its center. She was supposed to set a good example for the children. In addition, mothers were advised to set strict schedules for feeding and toilet training their children.

Middle- and upper-class families did not let their children work. For girls, childhood lasted from age two to twelve. Boys were considered children until they were fourteen. Both girls and boys were given toys that would help them grow appropriately feminine or masculine.

Girls were expected to play with dolls—either a newborn, introduced in 1910; a life-sized French-made doll called a *bebe*; or a stuffed Raggedy Ann, introduced in 1917. Teddy bears, named for President Theodore "Teddy" Roosevelt, were also popular.

Boys played with science and building kits. They built toy houses with Lincoln Logs, wooden blocks that interlocked. Or they might play with sleds in the snow or fight with toy swords. Some boys played with balls and bats. In the city, stickball, played with rubber balls and long sticks, was popular. Like boys today, they might follow sports statistics or collect baseball cards.

Not everyone, of course, had an easy childhood. Largely because of diseases such as cholera, typhoid, influenza, and tuberculosis, the average life span was only forty-seven. If they became ill or lost their jobs or farms, other parents found it impossible to support their families. Many children went to live with relatives. Still others lived on the streets or in orphanages. Mothers, both married and unmarried, unable to care for infants, often left them on the steps of hospitals. Since the mid-nineteenth century, abandoned children in New York City had been sent west to become adopted by new families. This program, managed by the Children's Aid Society, was called the "orphan train," after the trains that moved west carrying children to their new adoptive families. Up to 90,000 children were sent west by the time the program ended in the 1920s.

"Teddy bears" were named for President Theodore Roosevelt. (National Park Service)

Understanding Adolescence

In 1904, social psychologist G. Stanley Hall published a groundbreaking work. In it he introduced the idea of adolescence, a period in life between childhood and adulthood. The book was called *Adolescence: Its Psychology, and Its Relations to Physiology, Anthropology, Sociology, Sex, Crime, Religion and Education.*

The Young Women's Christian Association (YMCA) promoted good character and citizenship. This poster encouraged young women's efforts to support soldiers fighting in World War I.
(Library of Congress)

Before the twentieth century, youth had moved from childhood directly into adulthood. Many left school in the seventh or eighth grade. Boys went straight to work, and girls prepared for marriage. Now many young people went to school longer and married later. They had more time to get used to the many physical and emotional changes taking place in their bodies. Hall identified conflicts that these young people experienced. At first adolescence was a field of academic study, but it soon became accepted as a phase of life.

Adolescents became a focus of public attention. A new kind of school, the junior high, was created for them. Special organizations were created to give them a place to meet and to improve their character. Among them were the Young Men's Christian Association, the Young Women's Christian Association, Boys' Clubs of America, the Boy Scouts, and the Girl Scouts.

In his popular 1915 novel *Seventeen*, author Booth Tarkington called it the "time of life when one finds it unendurable not to seem perfect in all outward appearances." Nevertheless, adolescents continued to endure the awkwardness of uneven development that was common to their age.

Rising Divorce Rate

In colonial America, divorce was rare and often illegal. Economic survival outside a family, particularly for women, was almost impossible. Over time, however, laws were changed to make divorce possible. It also became easier for women to earn a living outside the home. Between 1880 and 1900, the number of women in the workforce doubled. By 1889, Americans were alarmed to discover that they had the world's highest divorce rate. How had this happened?

By now, public institutions had taken over many things that the family once did alone. Children were educated at school. The sick and mentally ill were treated in hospitals. There were special institutions for the aged and poor. The new family was still supposed to provide economic support for all its members and a safe environment for children. It was also expected to provide romance, companionship, and emotional satisfaction.

In 1889, there were almost 400 different legal reasons that people could get a divorce. All that began to change. By 1906, legislatures had tightened divorce laws in most states. There were fewer than twenty grounds for divorce now. New Jersey allowed divorce only on the grounds of adultery or desertion. New York recognized only adultery. South Carolina prohibited all divorces. In most states, courts required that every divorce identify a moral transgressor to be punished. The other spouse was assumed to be innocent and entitled to compensation. This often meant that women received alimony payments for life. If they were found to be at fault, however, they faced social disapproval and received no alimony.

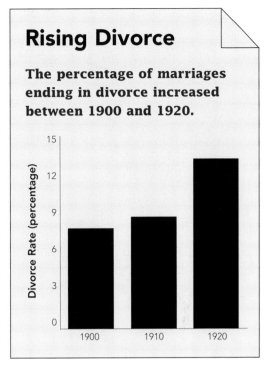

Rising Divorce

The percentage of marriages ending in divorce increased between 1900 and 1920.

Old Age

During the early twentieth century, the American population as a whole was getting older, as a result of an increasing life span and the declining birthrate. By 1920, the average age was 25.3. This may not sound old, but it was 20 percent higher than it had been fifty years before.

Studies showed that occupation, finances, and gender affected the lives of old people. Two-thirds of men over sixty-five still worked, because company-sponsored retirement pensions were extremely limited. Social Security would not become law until 1935. Most people considered a government old-age supplement anti-American and "socialistic." They did not believe that the federal government should be expected to spend money supporting the elderly. In some immigrant groups, one daughter in each family was expected to remain unmarried so that she might care for her parents.

On farms, older people might care for young children and in turn receive care from their families. In the city, there was less support for those unable to care for themselves. It would take time for the nation to address many of the social changes of modern family life.

Chapter Two

Social and Political Attitudes

President Theodore Roosevelt (LEFT); **Women marching in New York City** (RIGHT) **for suffrage, or voting rights.** (Library of Congress)

On September 4, 1901, President William McKinley arrived in Buffalo, New York, to visit the Pan-American Exposition. The exposition was a fair where nations of North and South America displayed their achievements. For the next thirty-six hours, the president gave speeches and appeared at patriotic displays. On the afternoon of September 6, he kissed a baby and was approached by a young man with a bandaged hand. A pistol was hidden inside the bandage. The man shot two bullets into the president's stomach. McKinley died eight days later.

The killing of President McKinley was the third U.S. presidential assassination in less than fifty years. Just twenty years earlier, in 1881, President James A. Garfield had been assassinated by a man who failed to get a job from the president. At the end of the Civil War in 1865, President Abraham Lincoln had been assassinated by a supporter of the Confederacy. All three assassins had grievances against the government. However, McKinley's assassin, Leon Czolgosz, from Poland, was the only foreigner and only anarchist. Like other anarchists, he thought that government was harmful and should be ended.

The killer's foreign background and radical politics made

some people worry about threats from other outsiders. Immigration laws were toughened. Social workers and labor leaders such as American Federation of Labor president Samuel Gompers supported them. They thought that fewer new immigrants would improve native workers' ability to get better wages and working conditions. Other social leaders worried about the nation's ability to absorb so many new immigrants from so many lands.

These thoughts carried little weight with big business. A major reason was that many business and factory owners welcomed immigration. More immigrants meant more low-cost labor. And big business was very powerful.

Big Business Rules

Just before Vice President Theodore Roosevelt took the oath of office as president, he spoke to the late McKinley's cabinet: "It shall be my aim to continue absolutely unbroken the policy of President McKinley for the peace and prosperity and honor of our beloved country." This calmed the cabinet. It also pleased industry leaders who controlled the railroads, banks, and factories. They thought Roosevelt would leave them alone to run the economy, as McKinley had. John W. MacKay of the Commercial Cable Company said about Roosevelt, "He knows just what we want and will do his best to shape things accordingly."

In the early 1900s, major services and products, such as transportation, oil, and steel, were controlled by trusts. A trust was a large corporation that combined many related companies so that it could control an area of business. Two of the most important were Standard Oil and U.S. Steel. Standard Oil was owned by John D. Rockefeller. It controlled nearly 85 percent of the U.S. oil industry. U.S. Steel was owned by Andrew Carnegie. The largest trust in the country, it controlled nearly all domestic steel manufacturing.

Trust owners said that the trusts were helpful because they reduced costs, which aided industrial expansion. Thinking that way, they were correct. Under the steel trusts, U.S. steel production increased by more than 100 percent between 1900 and 1910. But as fewer companies took control of more industries, it became clear that trusts hurt competition. In 1903, 1 percent of business controlled 40 percent of industry. Small companies were

John D. Rockefeller, owner of Standard Oil of Ohio (Library of Congress)

John D. Rockefeller's Standard Oil controlled almost the entire oil industry in the United States at the turn of the century. This cartoon compares Standard Oil to a giant octopus, gobbling up everything in its path. In one arm it is squeezing the U.S. Capitol building, home of the Congress, while another reaches for the White House. (Library of Congress)

driven out of business. These trusts were known as monopolies since they dominated, or "monopolized," American business.

President Roosevelt decided this was unfair and dangerous. During his first term he worked to bust, or break up, trusts he considered too powerful. He ordered government lawyers to work to dissolve the Northern Securities railroad trust, which controlled three major railroads. Applying an 1890s law called the Sherman Anti-Trust Act, they found that the corporation had too much control over the railroad industry. Northern Securities was dissolved, or broken up, in 1904. This pleased those who saw President Roosevelt as a protector of workers. However, many business owners were surprised and unhappy.

Over President Roosevelt's two terms between 1901 and 1908, there were forty-three other antitrust cases. Under his successor, William Howard Taft, there were ninety more antitrust cases between 1908 and 1912. Many big-business owners fought these cases but still supported the Republican party. The alternatives were less friendly to business. The Democratic Party supported antitrust laws and even more business regulation. Far less appealing to big business was the Socialist Party. That party challenged the idea of private ownership under capitalism. It wanted workers to control railroads, factories, and mines.

Public Irritation and the Progressive Era

By about 1905, there was much social unrest in the United States. Many Americans believed they were denied a good life by deep political and social corruption. President Roosevelt observed how upset some people were. He called it an "unhealthy condition of excitement and irritation in the popular mind."

There were many reasons for this discontent. Many families went hungry, while business tycoons had vast fortunes. Immigrants, African Americans, and others had difficulties in getting work and housing. Tens of thousands of children worked at dangerous and low-paying full-time jobs. Women were not allowed to vote.

In the early 1900s, nearly all Americans were affected by a troubled economy. There was almost continuous economic growth between 1900 and 1920. But the middle years of the period were complicated with financial problems. A panic in 1907 hurt business. It was followed by years of inflation. This was an increase in the supply of money, which lowered its value. Because money was worth less, the cost of necessities like food and housing increased. In part, inflation caused the cost of living to rise by 33 percent between 1908 and 1913.

Muckrakers and Reform Writing

Twentieth-century reform journalism began with a forward-looking magazine called *McClure's*. In 1901, its editor Samuel S. McClure sent writer Lincoln Steffens to visit big U.S. cities and investigate its politicians. A few months later, *McClure's* published Steffens's series "The Shame of the Cities." It detailed the huge political corruption in cities such as St. Louis and New York. In 1903, journalist Ida M. Tarbell wrote an exposé of the oil industry called *The History of the Standard Oil Company*. Her father had owned a small oil company that was destroyed by the oil trusts. Ray Stannard Baker wrote a tough analysis of the railroad trusts called "The Railroad on Trial," also published in *McClure's*.

President Roosevelt called this reporting muckraking. He meant the term *muckraker* to be somewhat critical. But the public and the writers themselves viewed it with approval. Muckrakers meant to bring social change. In the words of editor McClure, "Capitalists, workingmen, politicians, citizens—

all breaking the law, or letting it be broken. Who is left to uphold it? ... There is no one left; none but all of us."

However, the greatest public uproar and government response was provoked by a work of realistic fiction. It was Upton Sinclair's 1906 novel *The Jungle*. *The Jungle* was about the difficult life of a worker in the Chicago stockyards. Sinclair wrote about the unsanitary details of killing livestock. He showed how all parts of their bodies were used to make sausage and potted ham. President Roosevelt and the public were alarmed by such widespread unsanitary practices. They demanded change. In 1906, the Pure Food and Drug Act was passed to regulate the production and content of American-made food. These concerns created more demands for reform. A new political age, to be known as the Progressive Era, was emerging.

Political Protest Parties

The Progressive Era brought a wealth of new ideas and leadership. The power of the traditional Republican and Democratic parties was challenged, both within and by new parties. Protest candidates were elected to office, and their ideas became part of national thinking.

Eugene V. Debs, Socialist Party candidate for president (Library of Congress)

Socialism had first become popular in the United States during the nineteenth century. It was brought by European immigrants influenced by the teachings of Karl Marx. Marx believed that workers should control the economic production of a country. He taught that capitalism would destroy itself. In the first decade of the twentieth century, socialism was more widely tolerated by voters than in any decade in American history. Socialists were elected to many local offices. For example, in 1910, a Socialist was elected mayor of Milwaukee. Socialism gave a voice to some American workers who felt the Republican and Democratic political parties only spoke for big business.

The Socialist Party offered candidates for the presidential elections of 1904, 1908, 1912, 1916, and 1920. In most elections, the presidential candidate was Eugene V. Debs, a former railroad labor leader. He gained 3 percent of the votes in the 1904 and 1908 elections, and 6 percent in 1912.

The Populist, or People's, Party was more interested in reforming capitalism than destroying it. It tried to unite farmers and laborers throughout the country. William Jennings Bryan took many of the Populist ideas into the Democratic Party.

The Prohibition Party received about 2 percent of the vote in the 1904, 1908, and 1912 presidential campaigns. It supported national prohibition against alcohol.

The political party that had the greatest effect on a presidential election was the Progressive Party. Former president Roosevelt ran as a Progressive after he failed to take back the Republican nomination in 1912. The party was often called the Bull Moose Party, because of Roosevelt's claim that he felt as strong as a bull moose. Its platform included more regulation of trusts, suffrage (voting rights) for women, and an end to child labor.

Other Reform Leaders

Other reformers helped to make the early twentieth century a period of exceptional political, legal, and social leadership. Wisconsin Senator Robert LaFollette promoted Progessive ideas inside the Republican Party.

Another Progressive, Oliver Wendell Holmes, Jr., served on the Supreme Court from 1902 to 1932. Holmes became known as the Great Dissenter because he challenged the old view of the law as universal and unchanging. His opinions reflected the belief that law should reflect the needs of society. Attorney Louis Brandeis argued against monopolies and special interests before the Court. In 1916, he became its first Jewish justice. He and Holmes often agreed on social issues.

Louis Brandeis was the first Jewish justice to serve the Supreme Court. He was nominated by President Wilson in 1916. (Library of Congress)

Female leaders took up the cause of voting reform and direct social action. Alice Paul and Carrie Chapman Catt played central roles in gaining women's suffrage in 1920. Paul worked with suffragists in England and the United States and founded the National Women's Party. Catt was president of the National Woman Suffrage Association. In the late 1910s, the two persuaded President Wilson to make women's voting rights part of the war effort. Catt also worked for world peace throughout her life.

Charlotte Perkins Gilman was a leading feminist thinker. Two of her causes were building a common humanity and the

Alice Paul (LEFT) **and Carrie Chapman Catt** (RIGHT) **were two of the most important leaders in the fight for women's suffrage.** (Library of Congress)

need for women's financial independence. Jane Addams was an advocate for women and children. Hull House, the settlement house she started in 1889, became a model for social work. It was located in an immigrant neighborhood in Chicago and helped families adjust to their new homes.

Life under "Separate But Equal"

During the early twentieth century, life for African Americans became more difficult. The difficulties were caused by the 1896 Supreme Court ruling in the case of *Plessy* v. *Ferguson*. By an eight- to-one decision, the court ruled that it was not discriminatory to require black and white people to sit in separate train cars. The ruling came in a test case regarding New Orleans streetcars. However, once the court had ruled that "separate but equal" street cars were acceptable, segregation in every aspect of life became legal. Southern states passed more laws segregating hospitals, prisons, and even drinking fountains. Private businesses often had separate entrances for white and "colored" customers. In theory, if facilities were equal, they could be separate. However, facilities for whites were always better.

This segregation was informally known as Jim Crow laws.

Southern lawmakers promoted segregation as a peacekeeping tool. They said it would reduce white Southerners' fear that African Americans would take over southern politics and society. Instead, the laws gave African Americans second-class citizenship. Jim Crow laws prevented African Americans from voting, as they had since the end of the Civil War. Whites passed difficult requirements for literacy tests, poll taxes, and residency. By 1920, the number of African American voters had been greatly reduced. Unintentionally, Jim Crow reduced the South's power. That was because the South had fewer voters than it had in the 1880s. Population growth and new white women votes did not make up for the black voters lost.

During this time, the federal government did little to fight for civil rights. In 1903, President Roosevelt issued a public

Booker T. Washington founded the Tuskegee Institute, a college for African Americans. He is seen (THIRD FROM LEFT) with Robert C. Ogden (FAR LEFT), a trustee of the school, future president William Howard Taft (SECOND FROM LEFT), and business leader Andrew Carnegie (FAR RIGHT).
(Library of Congress)

W. E. B. Du Bois and the Niagara Movement

In 1903, a book by W. E. B. Du Bois called *The Souls of Black Folk* challenged established ideas about African Americans. Massachusetts-born educator William Edward Burghardt Du Bois, the first African American to receive a doctorate from Harvard University, argued that African Americans had been too narrowly focused on improving their economic condition. In so arguing, Du Bois attacked the most influential African American leader of the post–Civil War era, Booker T. Washington. Washington, a former slave, believed that African Americans' most important goal was economic autonomy, even if it meant accepting social inequality. A former supporter of Washington, Du Bois now believed that African Americans should be more concerned with working for political rights and ending segregation.

While many white and African American public leaders continued to support Washington's ideas, more militant thinkers sided with Du Bois. In 1906, Du Bois's supporters met on the Canadian side of Niagara Falls (they could not get lodging in the United States), to form a group and draft a statement. In it, they called for an end to discrimination in employment, union membership, educational choices, the justice system, and public places such as hotels and restaurants. This meeting marked the beginning of the Niagara Movement, which would be central to the development of a sense of urgency among twentieth-century African Americans to fight for equal rights.

W. E. B. Du Bois (Library of Congress)

Soon the Niagara Movement gained a wider following. White progressives such as reformer Jane Addams and philosopher John Dewey supported Du Bois's call for unconditional equality of the races. In 1909, white thinkers and African American members of the Niagara Movement met in New York. Borrowing from the ideals of the Niagara Movement, they founded the National Association for the Advancement of Colored People (NAACP). Over the next decades, it launched many campaigns for social and legal rights, and became the nation's leading civil rights organization. For years, its publicity director and editor of its journal, *Crisis*, was W. E. B. Du Bois.

letter condemning mob law and lynching. He also invited African American leader Booker T. Washington to dine at the White House. But he and other presidents during the period introduced no laws to aid African Americans.

Nevertheless, African American leaders continued their struggle. Ida B. Wells-Barnett crusaded against lynching relentlessly in Memphis, Chicago, and New York. W. E. B. Du Bois challenged Washington's willingness to accept white limitations. In 1905, he led a small group at Niagara Falls, to make a list of demands. Those demands included the right to vote and an end to segregation. In 1909, Du Bois was part of an integrated group that formed the National Association for the Advancement of Colored People (NAACP). He edited its journal, *Crisis*.

Reform and President Taft

Roosevelt did not run for a third term as president. After his victory in 1904, he made a statement that he would not run. In doing so, he followed an unwritten tradition among presidents of leaving after two terms. "We have had four years of uprooting and four years of crusading," said Roosevelt. "The country has had enough of it and of me."

Roosevelt chose Republican William Howard Taft to replace him. A quieter man than Roosevelt, Taft would have preferred a seat on the Supreme Court. However, he had little trouble defeating Democrat William Jennings Bryan. After Taft won, he pledged to follow Roosevelt's programs, much as Roosevelt had pledged to follow McKinley's. But, like Roosevelt, President Taft did not go along with many of them. His foreign policy was different. Unlike Roosevelt, Taft did not seek to become involved in the affairs of other nations. In 1911, he worked out a treaty that kept the United States and Britain from becoming involved in armed conflicts.

President Taft did not think of himself as a reformer, as Roosevelt did. When Congress refused his proposals, he did not use his executive power to pursue them. This made him more agreeable to big-business leaders, such as J. P. Morgan. Still, Taft oversaw several government reforms. Among them were the first national income tax, dozens of antitrust suits, and the Federal Children's Bureau to handle child welfare problems. Finally, in 1921, he was appointed to the Supreme Court, becoming the only former president to serve as chief justice.

Edging toward War

In August 1914, war began in Europe after months of increasing tensions. Because the war was 3,000 miles away, many people in the United States considered it a distant event that did not affect them. At first, President Woodrow Wilson supported this idea. He pledged U.S. neutrality.

In October 1914, the president announced a "Peace Sunday" to pray for "concord [agreement] among men and nations." Even after the Germans sank the luxury passenger ship *Lusitania* in 1915, killing 128 Americans, the United States remained neutral. But in that same year, President Wilson began to prepare for war. He approved military training camps and other war appropriations, or funds. He was beginning to agree with many U.S. leaders, such as former President Roosevelt, that the United States might enter the war.

One reason the country did not enter the war in Europe sooner was that it was involved in Latin America. It was continuing a plan that President Roosevelt began to protect American interests there. In the 1823 Monroe Doctrine, the United States had promised to stay out of Europe and warned foreign powers to stay out of the Americas. Now the United States added what became known as the Roosevelt Corollary (something that naturally follows) to that doctrine. The United States warned Latin America to keep its governments in order or risk U.S. police action. Between 1900 and 1917, U.S. troops intervened in Cuba, Panama, Nicaragua, the Dominican Republic, Mexico, and Haiti. The United States ended its Mexican involvement in 1917. It stopped looking for revolutionary and criminal Francisco (Pancho) Villa, who had killed several Americans.

The front page of the *New York Times* reports the news of the *Lusitania*'s sinking. (Library of Congress)

The Great War

In 1916, President Wilson, a Democrat, was reelected for a second term against Republican candidate Charles Evans Hughes. Hughes was a former New York governor and Supreme Court Justice. In part, Wilson was reelected because he had

President Woodrow Wilson was (CENTER) in a cheerful mood while at the first game of the 1917 American League baseball season. Later that year, he would reluctantly declare war on Germany. (Library of Congress)

avoided war. One of his campaign slogans was, "He Kept Us Out of War!" But events in 1917 forced the United States to enter the conflict. During February and March, German submarines sank four U.S. submarines. The British obtained a German document and gave it to the Americans. It was a letter from the Germans promising to help Mexico get back its old territories if it would form an alliance against the United States. The document became known as the "Zimmerman Letter," because it was sent by German foreign secretary Arthur Zimmerman. President Wilson took action. He told Congress that the United States must go to war to make the world "safe for democracy." On April 6, 1917, Congress declared war.

Two months later, a national draft began. Over 24 million men registered for military service by the end of the war in 1918. The War Industries Board regulated U.S. industries for the war. It made sure that industries like automobile manufacturers switched to wartime production. The government also raised funds by selling Liberty Bonds. U.S. citizens bought the bonds, which paid them interest on money they loaned the government. On average, Liberty Bond buyers spent about $400 each.

The End of the War

During the war, 2 million American soldiers, called Yanks by the Allies, crossed the Atlantic Ocean. They entered the war in its last year. The Americans were freshly trained and largely welcomed by other Allied troops. For much of 1918, they fought in France against Germany. Among U.S. battles were the fight to overtake Chateau-Thierry, the capture of St. Mihiel, and establishing a battle line in the Meuse-Argonne forest. Allied forces were set to cross the Rhine and invade Germany when the German government agreed to end the war. The armistice, or agreement, was signed on November 11, 1918.

While U.S. troops were praised abroad for helping end the war, President Wilson faced trouble at home. In February 1918, he introduced to Congress a long-term peace plan called the "Fourteen Points." The plan called for resetting European boundaries and establishing a "general association of nations" to settle problems. This association was called the League of Nations. President Wilson thought it was central to securing peace in Europe. It was to accompany the Treaty of Versailles, which was the peace treaty that Europe arranged.

Over the next year and a half, President Wilson and the Congress debated whether to approve the treaty and join the league. In fall 1919, the president toured the country to generate support for the League of Nations. In a September speech in Colorado, he said that the league could help the world move toward "the pastures of quietness and peace such as the world has never dreamed of before." But it would not happen. On October 2, 1919, President Wilson suffered a massive stroke and became partly paralyzed. The Senate did not approve the treaty or join the league.

In refusing to join the league, the United States followed a policy called isolationism. The nation aimed to remain free of economic and political relations with other countries. The United States wanted to avoid the problems created by the war in Europe. Among them were hunger, poverty, and economic unrest, especially in Germany. The United States wanted to focus on its own concerns. For more than a decade, it was able to do that.

Americans camped out in a shattered church during the battle of Argonne forest in France. Soon after the United States won the battle, Germany surrendered, ending World War I. (Library of Congress)

Then, in 1929, came the international crisis of the Great Depression. World War II followed ten years later. The United States was forced to end its isolation.

More Presidential Power

During the early twentieth century, the United States extended the vote to women and improved conditions for many workers. With prodding by reformers, the government curbed the extremes of big business. Progressive reforms shaped the government for the coming decades. But perhaps the most enduring change to the American government was made to the presidency.

In his two terms as president, Theodore Roosevelt increased the scope of presidential power. He made the job bigger. For example, he worked directly with labor leaders and business leaders like J. P. Morgan to end the 1902 coal strike. In so doing, he set an example that allowed government to become a partner in labor negotiations. This had never been done before.

Roosevelt was also bold in foreign policy. His slogan, "Speak softly and carry a big stick," meant that he did not hesitate to use U.S. military might. After leaving the presidency, Roosevelt argued for the United States to be more aggressive in international affairs.

Theodore Roosevelt also created the idea of the president as a larger-than-life personality. He was a great thinker who read 20,000 books and wrote fifteen. He was an adventurer who worked on ranches in the West and hunted wild game. He had been a hero in the Spanish-American War. When he was shot in the chest on a 1912 campaign stop, he refused to cancel his speech. He said, "I am very much uninterested in whether I am shot or not. It is just as when I was a colonel of my regiment." Roosevelt's presidency and image affected many presidents who followed him.

Theodore Roosevelt (Library of Congress)

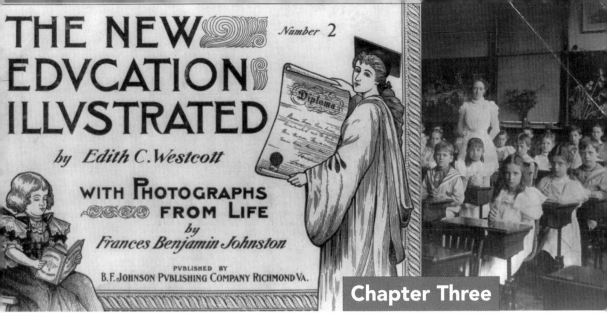

Chapter Three

Education

In the early twentieth century, several forces joined to reshape American education. One was the vast increase in students due to immigration. Another was the demand on curriculum (course of study) brought by industry. A third was the change in schools caused by city life.

The many thousands of immigrant children increased the need for all levels of schools. In response, hundreds of schools were built. Further, the schools' curricula, or the subjects and content taught, had to prepare students for an industrialized workplace. As the U.S. industrial output increased, business leaders pressed school systems to train students in skills needed for factory and office work. The industrial economy also created a need for new types of specialized education to prepare for high-level professions.

Educators tried to determine what all students needed to learn. This concern led them to create standards of various sorts. Among them were the setting of grade levels in primary and secondary schools and determining basic areas of study. Yet as some educators tried to make education more standardized, educational philosophers proposed to focus education according to a child's abilities.

Tension developed among business groups, educational philosophers, and policy planners who wanted education to instill American values. How these tensions were resolved created education in the twentieth century.

Photographer Frances Benjamin Johnston was one of the first well-known female photographers in the United States. Many of her turn-of-the-twentieth-century photographs of Washington, D.C. schools were collected in the book *The New Education Illustrated* (LEFT); one of the photographs from that book (RIGHT). (Library of Congress)

Before the Twentieth Century

In the nineteenth century, the United States developed schools that suited the country at the time. They were fairly small and mostly rural. Land ordinances in 1785 and 1787 allowed land to be set aside for public schools, which were built in many communities by the 1820s. But no plans for centralized school systems had been established. Nineteenth-century schools were usually one-room schoolhouses paid for by the community they served. Generally they had up to a few dozen male and female students from grades one to eight. One teacher, or school-master, taught all students, except when older students tutored younger ones. Until the mid-nineteenth century, most teachers were male.

The school curriculum was largely unregulated. Spelling, memorization, arithmetic, and values were emphasized. Popular mid-nineteenth-century textbooks included Noah Webster's *Spelling Book* and *McGuffey's Readers*.

Varieties of one-room schools were still being used in the early twentieth century. One man recalled his one-room school in the rural South around 1930 as "[one building] that had eight rows in it, one for each grade. Seven rows were quiet while the eighth one recited . . . . The woman teacher . . . taught every subject, and all eight grades . . . . " But for the most part, these schools

This one-room schoolhouse in Hecia, Montana was run by Miss Blanche Lamont (LEFT OF STAIRS). Children of different ages all sat in the same classroom. (Library of Congress)

Inside McGuffey's Reader

(Library of Congress)

Many early twentieth-century century schoolchildren learned to read and shaped their literary tastes in the same book other U.S. students had read for generations. It was McGuffey's "Eclectic Series" of readers.

The readers were compiled by college president and teacher William Holmes McGuffey in the 1830s. The First and Second Readers were published in 1837. There were at least five McGuffey Readers and several new editions by the early twentieth century. By then, 122 million McGuffey readers had been sold. The readers were translated into foreign languages and sent to countries including Japan and Puerto Rico to teach about American ways.

Like its earlier editions, the twentieth-century McGuffey's Reader offered examples of great literature, valuable information, and what its editors considered a healthy moral outlook. For example, the Sixth Reader contained 138 selections from 111 authors. These included nine excerpts from William Shakespeare, such as the soliloquy from the play *Hamlet*. Other writers included Henry Wadsworth Longfellow and Sir Walter Scott. There were also several selections from the Bible. For many generations, the readers were standard textbooks. As one man who read it as a child said, the Reader set "the very gates of literature ajar."

were phased out as school buses made it possible for students to travel to a central school.

Public high schools in the nineteenth century prepared students for college. They offered a classical curriculum of Latin, Greek, logic, and rhetoric (the art of writing and speaking effectively). Students who did not plan to attend college or seek white-collar jobs rarely attended high school. In 1890, 202,986 students attended 2,526 public high schools. By 1900, those numbers had nearly doubled. Almost 100,000 students graduated from high school that year.

End-of-the-Century Reform

The seeds that transformed education were planted in the late nineteenth century. In large part, lawmakers and educators reacted to increasing population and the growing number of industries that needed trained workers.

In 1873, it became easier for communities to fund public

Many education specialists in the early twentieth century believed that one purpose of school was to teach immigrant children "American values." This class in New York City included children from many countries.
(Calumet Regional Archives, Indiana University Northwest)

schools. The Michigan Supreme Court authorized the levying of school taxes to build and maintain community schools. The ruling opened a regular source of funding for elementary and high schools.

Meanwhile, various curriculum changes altered what was taught in school and how it was taught. By the late nineteenth century, some elementary school levels were divided into age groups. The first three grades might be grouped together, and the remaining grades were separated into another group. Emphasis remained on reading, writing, and arithmetic. In higher grades, students also learned literature, algebra, and specialized science courses.

As immigration increased the number and needs of students, educational leaders debated the purpose of high schools. Increasingly they believed that the role of the high school should be expanded. In addition to preparing students for college, it should also offer more practical choices. These choices would serve the wider needs of a larger population who might not attend college but needed education beyond primary school.

Late nineteenth-century educators agreed to establish a standard curriculum. It would ensure that students received a certain level of education, whether entering college or going to work. The National Education Association (NEA) appointed educators called the Committee of Ten. Led by Harvard University president Charles Eliot, the Committee of Ten recommended changes that set standards for schools and diversified what they taught.

The Committee recommended a standard twelve-year program. It included an elementary education of eight years and a secondary (or high school) education of four years. The Committee also suggested ways to modernize the high school curriculum, such as allowing students to take elective, or non-required, courses. The electives would stand in addition to required courses like English, foreign languages, history, and mathematics. The aim was to serve as many students' needs as possible.

Educating Young Children

Along with other reforms, a new education level was developed—the kindergarten. Introduced in Germany in the 1840s, it provided education for children aged three to seven. It was designed to stimulate the child's imagination and develop motor skills. The curriculum consisted of stories, play, crafts, and songs. Kindergarten was introduced to the United States in the mid-nineteenth century. But the first public kindergarten in the United States did not open until 1873, in St. Louis. American educators believed kindergarten was especially useful to immigrant families with two working parents. U.S. kindergartens came to offer a year's instruction prior to the first grade. By the early twentieth century, there were 225,000 kindergartens in America.

An Italian educator named Maria Montessori believed in the ability of young children to develop their minds on their own. In her native Italy, she developed a program of psychology, teaching methods, and teacher training. Together they allowed children to learn abstract concepts to develop their intellect at their own pace. In 1915, she brought her ideas to the United States. She was championed by leaders such as Helen Keller, who had gained fame for learning despite being both deaf and blind; and Alexander Graham Bell, the telephone's inventor and a speech therapist. Although Montessori schools would remain popular throughout the century, they remained primarily independent of public education.

Modern Elementary Schools

By the early twentieth century, most school systems had built upon the recommendations of the Committee of Ten. Elementary schools were divided into eight grades and taught basic reading, spelling, and arithmetic. They were centralized to serve children from several neighborhoods or districts. Larger schools were less expensive to run than many small ones. By 1920, many children rode to school on buses.

In each grade, students were taught a curriculum that became increasingly complex. Basic subjects included reading, writing, geography, and spelling. Memorization and drills were still used. For example, mastering a Shakespeare soliloquy was considered training for the mind. Penmanship was also stressed as a skill useful for office work. Although the fountain pen and the typewriter had both been invented in 1829, pens far outnumbered typewriters.

Helping students to be healthy and alert was another goal for schools. In many classrooms, there were mid-morning or mid-afternoon stretching exercises. In physical education classes, structured exercises were taught. In 1918, an international flu epidemic struck the United States. One out of four Americans eventually caught the life-threatening disease. Good health habits became vital.

As public-school students moved through the grades, they were taught to follow a standard set of rules for behavior. They were taught to go to school every day and to arrive on time. Although poorer districts could not afford full school days, the average school day ran from 8 A.M. to 4 P.M. The average number of days in the school year had increased from forty-five in 1870 to ninety by 1918.

To keep order, some teachers used corporal, or physical, punishment. They had various devices to discipline a child, including paddles and rulers. These items hung in the classroom to remind students of what happened if they disobeyed the teacher. Corporal punishment decreased as the twentieth century progressed.

Parochial and Other Schools

Parochial schools run by church parishes provided religious lessons in addition to basic subjects. During this period, the Lutheran and Roman Catholic religions were particularly active in building schools for their followers. American Catholic leaders set up rules for where their schools could be built and who could teach in them. The schools were built near the churches they served, and members of religious communities were the teachers. Textbooks were published by Catholic publishers and followed Catholic teachings.

Beyond Elementary School

By 1920, junior high school had become a part of American education. It was designed to teach students after they finished elementary school and before they entered high school. Depending on the school, it taught some or all of grades six through nine.

The number of high schools in the United States and students who attended them changed greatly. By 1920, there were 14,326 public high schools attended by 1,851,965 students. About 300,000 of those students graduated. High schools had several tracks of study, including college preparation, commercial business, drafting, and manual arts. Except in science labs, teachers lectured. Students were still expected to memorize and recite their lessons.

Hand in hand with the growth of high schools was a change in purpose. The National Education Association (NEA) refined its recommendations for high school subject areas. Published in 1918, the work was called the *Cardinal Principles of Secondary Education*. In it, the NEA said that high schools should offer education in seven basic subject areas. These included health, family life, vocation, citizenship, proper use of leisure time, ethical character, and basic activities like reading and writing. The aim of the expanded list was to promote the student's

A Job for Women

(Library of Congress)

Over time, teaching became a female profession. By the early twentieth century, 86 percent of U.S. teachers were women. School officials turned to hiring women because they could pay them less than men and because they were thought to present better examples for children to follow. The average teacher was twenty-five years old and was born in the United States. She had four years of schooling beyond elementary school and earned about $500 a year. Teachers were held to strict rules. In West Virginia during the 1910s, for example, teachers could not date or smoke, travel beyond the city limits without permission of the school board, or wear brightly colored clothing.

During the early twentieth century, girls often studied subjects like "household arts," which included cooking and cleaning instruction. This was especially true of girls from immigrant families, since many teachers assumed the girls would grow up to be maids. (Calumet Regional Archives, Indiana University Northwest)

personal development as well as make subject requirements. Most state school systems adopted these or similar guidelines for growth.

The Effects of Business on Education

Twentieth-century schools were not only shaped by education specialists but by American business ideals. These ideals of hard work and respect for time and money were tied into the curriculum. Just as the factory and office were made to run more efficiently, so were schools. Schools were seen as centers for work where students could be measured by their productivity. Depending on the level of schooling, that productivity could mean learning a list of spelling words, memorizing a poem, or completing a series of mathematical problems. Efficiency experts believed that organized learning would train the mind for the twentieth-century mechanized workplace. As turn-of-the-century historian Elwood Cubberly reported, the modern school could reasonably be seen as a factory.

To train students more completely for the mechanized workplace, some school systems developed vocational classes and vocational schools. By 1920, most schools offered courses in typing, stenography, bookkeeping, industrial arts, and agriculture. There were also schools devoted to practical or manual training. These courses were meant to prepare students for work that did not involve further specialized education.

New immigrants and African Americans usually attended these vocational schools. Among the most successful vocational programs was the school established for African Americans by Booker T. Washington. Beginning in the late nineteenth century and continuing into the twentieth century, schools such as his Tuskegee Institute in Alabama trained thousands of African Americans in the South. Washington's curriculum was designed to promote financial stability and the self-respect that followed from it. He felt that financial independence, more than civil rights, was most important for African Americans.

Washington's schools were praised and funded by northern white businesses. By the twentieth century, they were less well accepted by African Americans, who wanted to move beyond manual training and into academic and professional schools.

African American Schools

Many school systems barred African American enrollment. Southern schools were segregated by law by 1885. Because 85 to 90 percent of African Americans lived in the South between 1900 and 1920, black students suffered greatly.

Usually state-run African American schools were not as good as white schools. One reason was that African American school

An African American mother teaching her sons at home in the early twentieth century. (Library of Congress)

systems did not get the same amount of funds as white schools did. This was especially true in the South.

The government also spent its school money differently for the races. Money for white schools was used to create both academic and vocational tracks. For African Americans, state school systems set up only vocational training. General thinking among white social leaders was that African Americans were intellectually inferior to whites and could not follow an academic program. They decided what African Americans could learn. That meant carpentry or practical business for boys, and sewing and housekeeping for girls.

Some African Americans believed that African American children should learn more than just practical skills. Some of these adults taught students in their homes. Others established schools elsewhere, often with help from African American churches. Although some African American schools received donations from white educational foundations, donors usually gave to private schools such as Booker T. Washington's Tuskegee Institute, which only offered vocational training.

In time, the African American school attendance rate improved greatly. In the North, it matched or exceeded that for whites. For children ages ten to fourteen, for example, it rose from 50 percent in 1900 to about 70 percent in 1920.

Native American Schools

These Native American boys attended the Carlisle Indian School in Carlisle, Pennsylvania. The school was the first boarding school founded for Native Americans. The goal of schools like this one was to teach Native Americans to blend into American society. (Library of Congress)

Native Americans were educated differently from either white or African American students. Beginning in the nineteenth century, the U.S. government took an active role in their schooling. It did so because it wanted Native American students to give up their native ways and become Americanized, or as some clergy and government officials said, "civilized." To do this, the government separated Native American children from their families and traditions. In the words of the first Indian school founder, Richard H. Pratt, the goal was, "Kill the Indian and save the man!"

Beginning in 1879, Native American

children were forced to go to government-run schools. These included day schools, on or near the reservation or off-reservation boarding schools. The first boarding school was in Carlisle, Pennsylvania. It became a model for other schools in Kansas, New Mexico, and other western states. At these schools, the main goal was to force Native American children to assimilate, or blend into, white American culture. To do that, the children got English names and new clothing. Because the government believed they did not have the intellectual capacity for higher education, students were taught manual trades. They were not allowed to speak in their native language or talk to their parents. By the early twentieth century, more than 10,000 Native American children had gone to a government school.

The NEA protested that Native American culture was being destroyed. Early in the twentieth century, government officials saw that many Native Americans had not given up their native ways. Most resented being deprived of their families. The government moved the students back to the reservations and phased out the schools. In 1918, the Carlisle school closed. Native Americans were not granted U.S. citizenship until 1924.

Twentieth-Century Higher Education

For most Americans, higher education was a great luxury. Scholarships were few, and government student-loan programs had not been started. But one part of the modern college experience was in place. The College Entrance Examination was given for the first time in 1901. The idea behind the test came from Harvard University president and Committee of Ten reformer Charles Eliot. Then and now the test was designed to standardize college admissions throughout the nation.

Students at top universities such as Harvard or Yale were wealthy young men. Women were not admitted to many major all-male colleges until the late twentieth century. Instead they went to all-female colleges.

Nearly all students attending college in the early twentieth century were Protestants. As late as the 1920s, they made up nearly 90 percent of college students. There were strict limits on the number of Jewish students admitted. Most Roman Catholic students attended colleges and universities set up by their church in the 1890s.

Education and Democracy

John Dewey
(Library of Congress)

Philosopher John Dewey saw education as a way of practicing democracy. He was the foremost reformer in early twentieth-century America. In books that included *School and Society* (1899) and *Democracy and Education* (1916), Dewey developed his concept of education as an experimental process that could build people and communities, just as life in a democracy could do. Dewey taught that ongoing discussions among students and teachers were similar to citizens' debates on public issues. These ideas promoted education as a hopeful process central to maintaining democracy.

Other American reformers presented education as a way to gain greater representation in society. For example, social reformer Charlotte Perkins Gilman lectured in the United States and England about woman, education, and economics. Rather than promoting an educational program, she linked education to economic independence. Her best known book was *Women and Economics* (1898).

African American educator and activist W. E. B. Du Bois aimed to redirect African American educational policy and goals. In the early twentieth century, he rejected the vocational educational programs of Booker T. Washington. He charged that rather than make African Americans part of the educated world, such programs actually kept them uneducated and controlled by well-to-do whites.

Between 1900 and 1910, college attendance more than doubled. Institutions of higher learning also increased in number and type. Through United States land-grant laws begun in the last century, states acquired land and built hundreds of public colleges to offer technical and agricultural training. Those states whose schools admitted only white students were required by the federal government to start separate institutions for black students.

Since the end of the Civil War, almost all African American college students had attended segregated, all-black institutions. Some colleges, such as Lincoln University for men in Pennsylvania and Spelman College for women in Atlanta, offered a liberal-arts curriculum. Attendance also increased at all-black universities such as Howard in Washington, D.C., and Fisk in Nashville, Tennessee.

Junior colleges, which offered two-year college-level programs, also became popular. They were aimed at students who did not want or could not afford four-year institutions.

As students became more diverse, and as colleges oriented themselves more toward business and government, the purpose of college changed. By the 1920s, most college curricula focused on content-rich areas of knowledge, not on religious or moral training. They offered more modern courses, including psychology, sociology, and geography. More hard science and technology training was offered, in part to serve increasingly technological businesses. As they did in high school, electives became part of college curriculum.

Although many Catholic institutions struggled to survive, they would remain religious and apart from other colleges and universities until after World War II.

Universities expanded. Many with colleges and graduate programs started professional schools for law, medicine, dentistry, and theology. More schools opened for practical professions such as engineering, nursing, social work, and teaching. Between 1870 and 1910, the number of professionals in the U.S. workforce grew fourfold, to 1,150,000. By 1920, students were expected to get an advanced degree if they wanted to enter a specialized profession.

The Power of Education

As important as these advances were, they were not the main reason some people went to school. Many Americans simply had an inner desire to learn. They knew that education opened up a wider world. John Dewey linked education to democracy and to something greater. He said, "Education is not preparation for life; it is life itself."

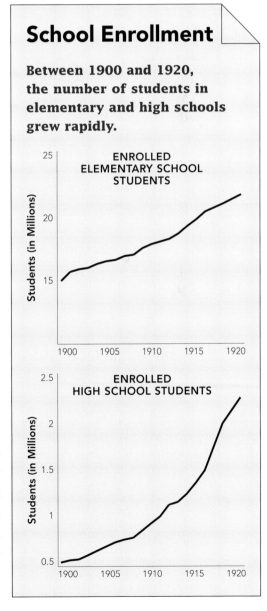

School Enrollment

Between 1900 and 1920, the number of students in elementary and high schools grew rapidly.

ENROLLED ELEMENTARY SCHOOL STUDENTS

Students (in Millions)

ENROLLED HIGH SCHOOL STUDENTS

Students (in Millions)

Chapter Four

The Economy

In the early twentieth century, the United States became a world economic leader, and its citizens became sophisticated and demanding consumers. Economic growth brought increased employment and productivity. With the growth of the automobile, railroad, and mining industries, U.S. businesses had a record number of jobs. Historic rates of immigration brought several million people into the country and a record number of workers. The workforce was about six times larger than it was in the nineteenth century.

These economic forces working together resulted in a growth in the Gross National Product (GNP). The GNP is a measure of the nation's entire economic production. It was growing at a rate of 3.6 percent a year. That was faster than European countries it traded with, including England. In 1910, the U.S. GNP was about $35.3 billion. By 1920 it had increased nearly threefold to $91.5 billion. The nation's output, or amount produced per worker, increased by 1.4 percent each year.

The U.S. economy would continue to grow throughout the twentieth century. But economic growth was not always even, and some industries declined. Between 1900 and 1910, there was a 30 percent increase in jobs. During the following decade, that increase slowed to under 10 percent. Railroad building and steel production had reached their highest point. In addition, the use of machines and greater worker efficiency had reduced the number of entry-level labor jobs.

Setbacks and Progress

The economy suffered great losses during the Panic of 1907. There were runs on some banks, and stocks fell in value. The panic was stemmed by a coalition of government and Wall Street forces. But a recession, or period of slow economic activity, resulted in lost jobs and reduced spending until 1908. A national depression, more severe than a recession, caused economic calamity in 1914. Several industries, such as textile mills, cut large percentages of their workers, and unemployment increased nationally. However, by 1915, international war-related business had restored the economy, which boomed until the late 1920s.

For the most part, the large number of workers kept wages level throughout the early twentieth century. Some industries kept wages low by having a constant supply of entry-level immigrant workers. For example, sweatshops where clothing was assembled and meatpacking firms continued paying low wages. Wages did not increase until 1915, when the Great War reduced the labor pool. Soldiers went to war, and workers left behind earned more. Farm prices stayed low until demand increased for food to feed troops at home and overseas.

Still, general working conditions improved throughout the early twentieth century. One improvement was the shorter workweek. In 1850, the average workweek was about sixty-six hours. In 1914, it was down to fifty-five hours. The average American worker made more money than workers in comparable jobs abroad. Even

Weekly Shopping List: 1901

The list below shows typical grocery items and their average weekly cost in 1901.

MEAT AND FISH

Four pounds of beef	48 cents
One pound of chicken	28 cents
One pound of fish	5 cents
One pound of ham	16 cents

EGGS AND DAIRY

Fourteen eggs	25 cents
One can of condensed milk	10 cents
Seven quarts of milk	70 cents

CEREAL

One package of breakfast cereal	10 cents
Twelve loaves of bread	60 cents
One package of crackers	10 cents
Flour	5 cents
Three dozen rolls	35 cents

VEGETABLES AND FRUIT

One pound of dried peas	5 cents
Fresh fruit	5 cents
Two quarts of potatoes	16 cents
One can of tomatoes	8 cents
Turnips, onions, etc.	10 cents

SUGAR, TEA, ETC.

Molasses (one pint per month)	3 cents
One bottle of pickles	10 cents
Three pounds of sugar	17 cents
One pound of tea	18 cents

ALCOHOL

Two pints of beer	20 cents

in 1900, the per-capita American income was $569, higher than for workers in other industrialized countries. The average salary rose to more than $600 per year by 1910 and grew steadily through 1920. Workers also got more for their money as the century progressed. From 1915 to 1926, earners' purchasing power increased 20 percent.

The Consumer Society

As the twentieth century began, the United States was a country of surplus resources for the first time in its history. It had more things than its people needed. More efficient industries and productive workers created more goods to buy. Economist Simon Patten wrote that this surplus would change American and world society completely. The change would produce *A New Basis of Civilization*, which was the name of a book Patten wrote in 1907. Sociologists and advertisers had a different term for it. They called it the *consumer society*.

In this new economy, businesses had to find creative ways to reach consumers with more money to spend on a greater choice of goods. Being at the center of a consumer society gave shoppers great power and responsibility. They had more types of stores to visit and more information from advertisers about more products to buy. They could purchase well-made, affordable products like the Ford Model T, and they could complain about products that were poorly produced. However, consumers also found that they sometimes needed the government's help to fight companies that made inadequate products. The early century heightened a practice of using government action to promote consumer safety. In these and other ways, consumers, businesses, and the government working together kept the modern economy going.

New Foods, New Packaging

The twentieth century transformed the foods Americans ate and the way they purchased them. In previous centuries, most Americans ate what they grew on the farm or bought in local towns. They had more choices by 1920.

One change was the year-round availability of fresh fruits and vegetables. Improved train and truck travel made fresh-food transportation possible. People learned new ways to prepare fresh produce. One was the California style of making salads of fresh fruits and raw vegetables.

Prepared foods also grew more popular as the pace of people's lives grew faster. As more people worked at nonfarming jobs away from home, they relied on train and trolley schedules to get to work on time. Multicourse breakfasts took too long to prepare and eat. Kellogg's Corn Flakes and Quaker Puffed Rice became popular in the 1910s. They were promoted by cereal developers, like the Kellogg brothers, who spoke to groups across the country about the benefits of a "health food" breakfast of cereal.

Fruit cocktails and Campbell's soups were among the early successes in canned foods. Both were introduced in the 1910s. Frozen vegetables and meats also began showing up in grocery stores. First produced by Clarence Birdseye, frozen foods tasted fresher than those stored in cans. As more people got freezers in the 1920s, frozen foods became even more popular.

Another popular food advance in the 1910s was prepared condiments, such as Hellman's mayonnaise and Morton's salt, which poured freely and could be used at the dinner table.

Mass-produced sweets became popular too. Chocolate bars introduced by Pennsylvania chocolate maker Milton Hershey were promoted as sources of quick energy. They were seen as a particularly useful food for the military during World War I. A

Chocolate maker Milton Hershey first began selling his famous Hershey's Kisses in 1907. (Hershey Community Archives)

Piggly Wiggly became America's first supermarket when it opened in 1916. (Courtesy of Piggly Wiggly, Inc.)

circular, hard, peppermint candy with a hole inside called the Life Saver was introduced in 1912. It was an immediate success. Popular cookies introduced in the early twentieth century included the Oreo chocolate sandwich cookie and the Lorna Doone shortbread cookie.

New Food Markets

As more varieties of food became available, so did the places to buy them. One was the self-serve market called the "combination store," or the grocery store. Before the twentieth century, people purchased foods from specialized salesmen such as butchers, fishmongers, or fruit peddlers. A clerk filled each customer's order with items stored behind the counter. Clerks listed the costs on a tab, which the customer paid every week or month.

The first grocery store was the Piggly Wiggly, which opened in Memphis, Tennessee, in 1916. Founded by Clarence Saunders, it allowed customers to walk through the store and choose what they wanted. The Piggly Wiggly was an immediate success. It was followed by other similar grocery stores across the country. The grocery store changed food shopping forever. Going to the market became quicker and more independent. It also became a cash-only activity.

Like food preparation and grocery shopping, restaurant dining became simpler and faster. Restaurants that served quickly prepared food became popular. Inexpensive lunch and dinner restaurants called "chophouses" had limited selections and could serve food quickly. An early example of a fast-food stop was Nathan's hot-dog stand, which opened at New York's Coney Island amusement center in 1916. These restaurants paved the way for fast food places that grew in large numbers in the twentieth century.

The Department Store

Shopping for clothes and household items was also more streamlined. This was the aim of the department store, where many types of items for the entire family could be purchased. The 1877 announcement for the first John Wanamaker department store in Philadelphia claimed it answered the public's "call for such a central and extensive point for shopping." Besides Wanamaker's, early department stores included Macy's and Gimbel's.

By the twentieth century, many Americans were used to department stores. In 1920, there were about 1,000 of them across the country. City officials liked department stores because they helped to show a city's sophistication. Like movie palaces and skyscrapers, department stores demonstrated that a city was important enough to support big businesses. Department stores often featured the latest architecture. For example, Chicago's Marshall Field's and Boston's Filene's were designed by leading architect Daniel Burnham.

The department store also provided many types of entertainment. Greeters helped ladies from their vehicles. Organ or piano music played all day. Sculptures rose from the middle of the selling floor. Some stores had miniature flower gardens, and one had a petting zoo. There were also seasonal sales for holidays and for certain kinds of goods. For example, sheets, towels, and tablecloths were sold at white sales in January. Some stores, such as Filene's, set up bargain basements to sell leftover items at low prices.

Window Shopping Memories

In some cities, parts of streets became known for their shopping. In Chicago, department store shopping was done on State Street. In New York CIty, shopping was done along 14th Street, which had so many stores for women that it became known as Ladies' Mile. Shopping—and window shopping— was also done along New York's Broadway. As immigrant Mary Antin recalled, it was an exciting Saturday night activity to "march up Broadway and [take] possession of all we saw...or desired."

Ordering by telephone became popular among some buyers. Department stores gave special service to customers making telephone orders. They knew that customers making telephone orders were probably wealthy, since many people still could not afford to have telephones in their homes.

To find more inexpensive items and treats, many Americans went to the five-and-ten-cent store. The earliest of these stores had been founded in the 1870s by businessman Frank Woolworth. By the 1910s, there were about 600 Woolworths stores. Many had low-cost lunchrooms too. "Five and dimes" stocked thousands of everyday items such as clothes, health and beauty products, stationery, and toys. Because the prices were so low, Woolworth believed customers sometimes bought things "on the spur of the moment." This practice became known as "impulse buying." It became a cornerstone of many other businesses as time went by.

The arrival of the Sears, Roebuck catalog was especially exciting for Americans living in rural communities. Some of those who lived in the country-side had to travel long distances to do shopping for the kinds of goods sold in the calalog. The only way for many rural people to purchase some of the items was directly from the calalog.
(Private collection)

Peddlers and Catalogs

While department stores and five-and-ten-cent stores attracted modern shoppers, some people still bought from street peddlers. These peddlers were often recent immigrants to cities or traveling salespeople who served rural communities. In cities, peddlers sold daily necessities like milk or ice. They also sold specialty items like jewelry and women's undergarments. In 1905, a dealer began a door-to-door sales program known as Fuller Brush. Housewives could buy brushes and other cleaning items when a salesman came to call.

Many rural and small-town customers favored shopping by the mail-order catalogs. Usually people filled out an order form, mailed it in, and waited for delivery by mail. At Christmastime, the catalogs were known as wish books, because children poured over them and picked what they hoped Santa would bring. By 1910, about 10 million Americans were catalog customers. Companies like Sears, Roebuck and Montgomery Ward & Company mailed out thick catalogs that sold thousands of items. Sears called itself "The Largest Retail Supply House in the World." Its 500-page catalog included hammers, corsets, underwear, toys, and guns. Sears even sold do-it-yourself houses.

In some small towns, local businesses set up promotions to discourage customers from mailing away business. The promotions stressed the importance of supporting local shopkeepers.

Advertising Takes Charge

Hand in hand with new markets for consumers were the new ways to communicate with them. Advertising became a powerful and successful business during the early twentieth century. In 1900, advertisers spent $95 million per year to sell their products.

This 1907 photograph of Second Avenue in Seattle illustrates the growth of advertising during the early twentieth century. Large billboards, like the cigar advertisement seen here, were becoming common city sights. (Library of Congress)

By 1920, they were spending more than $500 million.

Advertisers learned ways to make people buy. They studied late-nineteenth-century psychologists like William James to figure out how to change people's thinking. They used signs and images to create a demand for a product. They hoped to convince people they needed a certain product, even if they did not.

Colorful displays were particularly popular in country stores where customers did not have daily newspapers to provide advertising. For example, seed companies showed color pictures of the flowers their seeds would yield.

In cities, readers learned about fashion trends in daily newspapers. Big department stores like Macy's and Wanamaker's placed fashion advertisements in the women's sections of the newspapers.

Women also learned about household consumer trends in magazines. Magazines did not accept advertising until the turn of the century. By the 1910s, magazine advertising had taught people to recognize certain products and to ask for them by brand name. Outdoor advertising also promoted prepared foods, health remedies, and other brand items. Billboard advertisements appeared along train routes, on streetcars, and on buildings.

Specialized Markets: Women and Youth

Women emerged as the nation's major consumers. By 1920, sales studies showed that 90 percent of all spending in the United States was controlled by women. Even if a man purchased an item, it was in some way influenced by a woman. As one newspaper publisher explained, it was part of the "chain of matrimony" to have the female decide what to buy. So the businesses aimed their advertising at women. In magazines like *Ladies Home Journal*, companies spent about $70 million to guide women in their decisions on buying everything from facial soap to automobiles.

Youth formed another major new market in the early twentieth century. Activists and politicians proclaimed 1909 to 1919 as the "Decade of the Child." As they celebrated laws against child labor and for compulsory schooling, advertisers saw a new category of consumers. During the 1910s, more advertisements featured youthful faces. These faces appeared in ads for traditionally adult products like toothpaste, facial soap, and makeup.

During the Great War, government advertisements used a patriotic and stern poster of Uncle Sam to convince young men to serve their country.

Spending to Celebrate and Feel Good

Before the twentieth century, most holidays were celebrated locally and quietly. Now advertisers and businesses made holidays more commercial. Holidays that were fundamentally religious, like Christmas, or patriotic, like the Fourth of July, became consumer events. New holidays were even created during the period. Among them were Mother's Day and Father's Day, both of which were founded in the 1910s.

This famous advertisement for the U.S. Army was created by James Montgomery Flagg to encourage young men to report for service in the army during World War I. (Library of Congress)

American consumers celebrated the holidays in many ways. They had begun to send greeting cards in the late nineteenth century. Brightly printed Christmas cards usually showed Santa Claus, snow scenes, or holy images. Birthday cards had writing and festive imagery. Sending cards came to be considered good etiquette.

Stores and advertisements refined some holidays into seasons. During the holiday season, there was a period of days or weeks when certain items were displayed and sold. For example, Christmas displays at rural stores had inexpensive items like toys for children, perfumes for women, and guns for men. At department stores, there were lighted figurines and window displays that told stories. These got people interested in buying more gifts.

Early twentieth-century advertisements suggested that social goals could be met by consuming. Many Americans associated their purchases with popularity. They became more interested in cleanliness and good grooming. Women bought soap that gave them what one ad said was "the skin you love to touch." They went to the beauty parlor to have their hair done. They made themselves beautiful with lipstick and rouge.

Men became clean-shaven after the Great War. The military had distributed advertisers' free samples of safety razors and disposable blades during the war. Men were encouraged to shave off beards and moustaches. After the war, they kept shaving. Men and women both brushed their teeth with toothpaste. By the mid-1920s, they used mouthwash to ward off the new stigma of "halitosis," or bad breath.

Critics of Consumers

As more Americans became active consumers, social critics found fault with them. Some criticized Americans for believing that the items they bought made them important members of society. A leading critic of American consumer life was Thorsten Veblen. Born in the Midwest, Veblen became known for his 1899 book *The Theory of the Leisure Class*. In it, Veblen wrote his theories about economics. But the ideas that stuck in popular thinking were his description of the part of society that depended on money. It was called the leisure class. People got status from the amount of money and spending power they had. In little and big ways, they spent money so that people could see that they had money. This might mean fancy houses, clothes, cars, vacations. Veblen called this kind of spending *conspicuous consumption*. The term is still used today.

In the 1920s, the voices of the critics got louder, but they were drowned out by the sound of cash registers ringing up more consumer goods. Although social critics may have been correct, there was no way to answer the overwhelming desire many felt at the thought of new things. Immigrant Mary Antin was captivated by the "dazzlingly beautiful palace called a 'department store'," and the immigrant daughter in Anzia Yezierska's novel *The Bread Givers* counters her mother's belief that America does not have the beautiful handmade things "like we had home." The daughter cries in disagreement, "Nonsense, Mamma! . . . If you only had the money to go on Fifth Avenue you'd see the grand things you could buy." It was an excitement that carried through America's twentieth century and into the next.

Chapter Five

Work

Work changed in the United States during the early twentieth century. Jobs grew about 30 percent between 1900 and 1910. This growth was tied to increased industrialization. Railroads added tens of thousands of miles of track, and steel production increased at historic rates. The gross national product, which measures the nation's total output, nearly tripled between 1910 and 1920. It grew from $32.3 billion to $91.5 billion.

Cities and small towns became dotted with factories, mills, and work camps. In the Detroit area alone, the automobile industry rose from less than 10,000 jobs to more than 200,000 between 1900 and 1920. These workers produced over 15 million Ford Model T cars. Automobile workers were mostly male, but at other sites, women and children worked too. In some jobs, like store clerking or newspaper hawking, they held almost all the jobs.

Increased industrialization made many investors and business owners wealthy. Among the richest were tycoons such as oilman John Rockefeller and automaker Henry Ford. Outrage over these large fortunes led to the passage of the first federal income tax. The Constitution was amended in 1913 to make it legal.

Owners and managers tried to keep the workplace productive through strict rules and long hours. Workers largely kept pace with employer goals. At the same time, they rebelled against attempts to dehumanize the work experience. Over time, they

During the first two decades of the twentieth century, many jobs were done by children, sometimes as young as five years old. In the photograph above (LEFT), a group of young boys pose outside of the coal mine where they worked. (Library of Congress) When the United States entered World War I, many jobs that had typically been done by men, such as operating a railway mail parcel truck (RIGHT), were done by women. (National Archives)

came to see their position as opposed to that of the managers and owners. This led to record numbers of union members and to labor-management clashes. Strikes and demonstrations flared at sites ranging from mills in Massachusetts to mines in Colorado. These demonstrations, along with the pleas of social critics brought about much on-the-job reform. Still, for most laborers, the workday was long and oppressive. As one Brooklyn garment factory worker reported in 1902, "The machines are all run by foot power, and at the end of the day one feels so weak that there is a great temptation to lie right down to sleep."

Farming and Agriculture

As industry created new jobs in towns and cities, farm jobs shrank. The farmer remained an ideal in American art and popular thinking. But the number of people who made their living by farming decreased significantly. In 1870, farmers represented almost half of the workforce. By 1920, farming accounted for only 27 percent.

Most small farms were family operations that hired a few seasonal workers. The main jobs were done by family members, and this work changed only when the family bought new machinery, such as a modernized combine, an automatic harvesting and threshing machine. Crops raised on the farm varied by region. In the South, it was cotton or tobacco. In the Midwest, it was wheat and corn. Life on the farm followed a year-long season of planting, harvesting, and auctioning the crop for the family's annual earnings.

Most independent rural farmers considered themselves middle class. Generally, small rural farms did not grow into agricultural business enterprises. They yielded enough crops to sustain one family. But there was not enough land to break up into portions for their grown children. Some farmers purchased adjacent farms and hired them out to tenant farmers. If a growing city expanded toward a farm, the land might be sold to real estate developers.

By the early twentieth century, many farmers did not own the land they worked. The rising cost of farming and economic depressions put ownership out of reach. Tenant farmers, or sharecroppers, who worked land owned by someone else, were often from ethnic minorities. Many were African Americans who had once been enslaved. They rented land and housing and shared a

A family farm in Owyhee County, Idaho in about 1906. (Library of Congress)

portion of the money from the crops with the landlord. Often they were charged by their landlords for food and supplies. Generally tenant farmers made just enough to live on and were not considered permanent members of their communities. Some hired hands drifted from place to place to provide seasonal labor on farms in states with abundant crops, like California.

An increasing number of farms were enterprises of thousands of acres owned by financial speculators and out-of-town businessmen. To these groups, the farm was a business that raised crops that were either specific to their region or that had a sure-fire market, like hops for beer or wheat. Known as "bonanza farms," they were often located in rich growing regions like Nebraska and California. They were run by a manager who oversaw dozens of farm laborers. He ran a military-type operation that featured the most up-to-date farm equipment. Its specific goal was to make money for the owners.

In fact, due to this improved labor-saving equipment, large farms were more productive. While the number of farms and farmers decreased, yields of staple crops such as wheat, corn, and cotton increased 150 percent over the previous thirty years. In particular, productivity increased to fill the demands of World War I.

Throughout the period, two images of the farmer persisted. One was the nineteenth-century independent farmer, whose image was reproduced in lithographs and paintings. The other was the rich businessman farmer that novelist Frank Norris visualized in his 1901 novel *The Octopus.* Each appealed to a different version of the American dream.

Loggers in Clallam County, Washington.
(Library of Congress)

Nonfarm Labor

Some workers cultivated the land away from farms. These jobs included logging, mainly in the Northwest, or coal mining, particularly in Pennsylvania. For example, in the coal mine there were many jobs, including extracting coal from the mine, inspecting the coal, and removing refuse. Coal miners worked various levels, or gangways, deep in the mine. There they used blasting powder to loosen coal from the mine wall. The coal was then gathered into a cart or buggy and moved by track and elevator to the top of the mine.

Surrounded by water, coal gases, and continually falling coal, mine workers faced many injuries. Among them was exposure to methane, carbonic acid, and other gases, which caused lasting harm. Also deadly was black lung disease, which was caused by inhaling coal dust. Most mines were owned by distant corporate syndicates (associations), not independent owners. They were managed by barn bosses who controlled various areas of the mine.

Industrial Plant and Mill Work

American workers engaged in a wide variety of manufacturing, service, and clerical jobs. These jobs were available in nearly every big city and small town. They were marked by increasing innovation, efficiency, and work times that were governed by the clock rather than natural daylight. By 1900, two-thirds of Americans worked in industries regulated by the time clock. African American factory workers were given the less desirable jobs and were paid less than white workers in the same position.

Mills and plants put mass production into practice in various ways. At manufacturing plants, workers took on one part of a larger, centralized process, like packing food into cans. Many items produced in factories, like tomato ketchup, had once been made at home. With mass-production techniques, the items were less expensive to produce than they would be if made by hand.

Another common labor site was a large-scale mill. Mills employed hundreds of workers and processed lumber or textiles. Typically they were owned by a single family and located in New England or the South. They were located near a body of water for power and trade. Often they served as a nucleus for a town, or else they were set off in a mill district of a major industrial city, like Cincinnati.

In the twentieth century, however, the industrial plant surpassed the mill as the main site of manufacturing. In many ways, it suited the larger, more mechanized workplace. The plant was often owned by outside investors, not a family. It employed larger numbers of people, often thousands, as in the Ford plant outside Detroit. Rather than create a town, the plant developed an industrial hub that attracted housing developments and railroads.

As electricity came into use, it speeded up the work process. Industrial jobs were increasingly subdivided, so a worker may have only a small portion of a product to construct or inspect. As a result, he might not know the final product being made. As plants became more modernized, machines took the place of workers, and many jobs were eliminated.

Also influential in the early twentieth-century workplace was

Inside the Ford Motor Company factory in Highland Park, Michigan. (Library of Congress)

the efficiency expert. He suggested ways to restructure time, tasks, and space to increase efficiency. Among the best-known was Frank Gilbreth. He pioneered time-saving devices to perform multiple tasks with one movement and produced more efficient factory floor space.

Manufacturers developed various improvements for assembling complex items. Conveyor belts moved grain or iron as they were processed. In slaughterhouses, teams worked in sequences to butcher animals. These refinements went into the landmark development of the chain-driven assembly line for Ford automobiles in 1913 and 1914. Debuted at the plant in Highland Park, Michigan, the line could assemble an automobile chassis in just over ninety minutes. Three such assembly lines were in use at Ford by 1914. The repetition and constant movement of the line caused many workers to quit.

Founder Henry Ford surprised the business and working worlds by raising pay to $5 per day and reducing the workday to eight hours. The daily pay rate was twice what industrial workers were usually paid. The higher wage was meant to keep workers from leaving in large numbers. It stabilized the workforce on the assembly line.

Like coal and logging sites, mills and plants were sources of many injuries. In 1913, it was estimated that some 25,000 workers had died in industrial accidents, and 70,000 were seriously injured. The workplace came to be viewed as a ground of danger where workers and management confronted each other.

Women at Work

In the first decade of the twentieth century, female participation in the American workforce rose from 23.5 to 28.1 percent of all workers. Women sustained this level of employment for the next two decades. They improved the types of jobs they obtained and the social respect they earned. Thanks to the founding of women's colleges such as Smith in the late nineteenth century and the opening of some all-male public and private institutions to women, higher education was more widely available.

Largely, though, women worked at various service jobs. Elementary school teaching had become a female stronghold in the late nineteenth century. Now it extended into the secondary schools. In addition, women entered the office as secretaries and the

Switchboard operators, nicknamed "Hello Girls," at work at Chesapeake
and Potomac Telephone Company in 1920. (Library of Congress)

sales floor as clerks. In particular, the sales job represented a change
in social attitude that made the regular presence of women in highly public places like stores acceptable. In fact, by 1900, women completely dominated department store sales-clerk positions. They were
considered by department store owner John Wanamaker as having
"more tact and accuracy" than men. Women also held managerial
and marketing positions in the department store.

One occupation defined by women almost from its outset
was the telephone operator. "Hello Girls" worked the switch-
boards, providing connections for the phones that grew from 1.3
million in 1900 to 13.3 million in 1920. Although initially men
were hired as operators, they were found to be unreliable and
argumentative. Instead, women adapted to the regimen of polite-
ness, speed, and organization, answering each call with,
"Number, please?" and tending to requests to call at certain times
allowing the receiver to make a train or wake up from a nap. As
the New York Telephone Company said in 1912, the operator
was "The Voice With a Smile."

Female college graduates often became social workers, and
they dominated the field. In 1910, one of them, Julia Lathrop,
became the first female head of a federal agency when she was
appointed by President Taft to head the Children's Bureau. An
increasing number of women became medical doctors during the
period, the gender accounting for 20 percent of the profession by

1920. Similarly, the number of female nurses in the United States increased sevenfold.

Throughout the era, women encountered public disapproval for abandoning their "correct" place in society by leaving their homes to work and competing with men for money. For example, one 1910 novel portrayed its working-girl character as someone with poor manner who never went to church, while her mother "blushed with embarrassment."

Yet during World War I, women assumed a wider range of jobs. They were hired as secretaries more often than ever, hastening the replacement of male secretaries. The American Federation of Labor acknowledged this trend when it accepted females for union membership as secretaries. Although women were generally not hired for jobs in heavy industry, they drove trucks and maintained farms for the war effort. More than 5,000 served as army nurses overseas, and another 20,000 served in the armed forces, primarily as clerks and secretaries.

Scientific Management

The influence of science in the late nineteenth century led social scientists to believe scientific techniques could be applied to everyday life. Of particular interest was the workplace. There it was believed that workers could become more efficient by matching their actions to those of the machines at which they worked. In addition to moving the body to coordinate with the actions of a machine, tasks were divided into the same portions performed by a machine.

A foremost proponent of scientifically influenced time management was Frederick Winslow Taylor. In his 1911 book *Principles of Scientific Management*, Taylor outlined the time and motion techniques that he asserted could cut down on excess motions and distractions that wasted work time. Taylorism, as the time-saving process came to be called, rested on four concepts: (1) the setting of a standard work rate by testing with a stop watch, (2) the setting of work phases that could be monitored by time clocks, (3) the training and monitoring of workers for each task, and (4) the paying of workers according to their performance as marked on the time clock.

In offices, time-saving techniques included redesigning the worker's desk. Instead of the rolltop desk, which ensured privacy, many twentieth-century offices had a variation of the Modern Efficiency Office, which debuted in 1915. The flat desk had drawers that could be easily checked by managers and no room for personal items or decorations.

Time management appealed to a public whose everyday life had been speeded up by the telephone, telegraph, and mass transportation. Most workers accepted some parts of scientific management but fought against others. Time clocks and punch cards were standard in mills, factories, and offices. But workers fought working under the clock in various ways, including holding short surprise strikes.

Unions Grow as Tension Mounts

The social and economic gap between workers and management widened. There were many reasons. One reason was the high percentage of workers born outside the United States who were unfamiliar with English and lacked an advocate. In 1900, one-third of the industrial workers were immigrants. Low wages put another wedge between workers and managers. For example, in 1909, 40 percent of laborers lived below the poverty line of $660. During an average year, laborers also faced sizable unemployment. In any year, about 25 percent of the industrial workforce was employed for only part of the year. Moreover, management often increased productivity by requiring workers to adopt a faster pace or replacing them with machines. In nearly all ways, the aims of owners clashed with those of workers. Unions mediated between them, since they represented a mass of workers and showed their collective strength and usefulness to the owners.

Early twentieth-century union membership grew among both agricultural and industrial workers. The union with the largest membership was the American Federation of Labor (AFL), headed by Samuel Gompers. Between 1900 and 1910, it grew from 548,000 to over 1.5 million members. By 1917, the AFL had 3 million members, and in 1920, following the production boom brought by World War I, it had 5 million members. Through much of the era, Gompers sought government cooperation to improve the union's lot. In particular, he wanted unions to be exempt from antitrust laws. Ultimately, in 1914, he was able to negotiate partial exemption with the passage of the Clayton Antitrust Act.

Samuel Gompers, leader of the American Federation of Labor
(Library of Congress)

State militia confront strikers in Lawrence, Massachusetts, during a 1912 textile mill strike. (Library of Congress)

In nonurban areas and the western states, unions such as the United Mine Workers (UMW) and Industrial Workers of the World (IWW) organized workers. Led by Big Bill Haywood, the IWW, or "Wobblies," represented miners, lumberjacks, and others early in the century. In the next years, the IWW moved eastward and represented textile workers. The IWW became known for using violence to achieve its goals. Haywood and others stood trial for violent acts in 1907 and 1911. The IWW led widely known strikes of textile workers in Paterson, New Jersey, in 1913 and Lawrence, Massachusetts, in 1912.

Unions were involved in strikes and subsequent acts of violence at record rates. Among the hundreds of strikes that took place were the IWW action against the Wheatland Ranch in California in 1913 and the UMW's stike against the Colorado Fuel and Iron Company in Ludlow, Colorado, in 1914. This strike ended with the deaths of thirty-nine workers and children at the hands of state and federal militia.

Child Labor

As the century began, children constituted one-sixth of all workers nationwide and one-third of all workers in the South. They began working as young as age three, usually at home in sweatshop-type labor. Most children outside the home were employed in low-paying, unregulated areas like domestic work, mill work, and street labor. Foe example, a child might make artificial flowers or sell newspapers. Children were needed mainly to work to add to the working-class family's income.

Although some states had legislation protecting the right of children to obtain an education, there were several loopholes. Employers provided waivers that the parents signed, or they obtained false proofs of identification.

From the beginning of the twentieth century, social reformers made the regulation and even elimination of child labor a main goal. The reformers charted the physical dangers to working children in factories and even at home, where labor might involve poisonous paints or harmful repetitive motions, such as cigar rolling.

In 1904, reform efforts led to the formation of the National Child Labor Committee. It set state standards for minimum age and maximum working hours per day per child. State offices were also established to ensure that these regulations were followed. However, there was no regulation requiring states to adopt the rules. Many did not. Factories mounted intensive lobbying efforts to convince Congress that additional regulation of child labor was not needed.

Yet reformers continued to press for more government regulation of children's work laws. After 1914, the National Child Labor Committee joined forces with another government-backed agency, the U.S. Children's Bureau, part of the U.S. Department of Commerce. In 1916, Congress responded to the reformers' calls and passed the Keating-Owen Law. The law imposed far-reaching standards and regulation over many types of previously unregulated businesses in which children worked. For example, it prohibited the hiring of children between fourteen and sixteen years of age and made it illegal to move items from shops employing children aged sixteen or under. Although the bill was initially rejected by the Department of Commerce–backed National Child Labor Committee and President Wilson, the bill was passed. Ultimately, in a 1918 United States Supreme Court ruling on the case of *Hammer v. Dagenhart*, the Keating-Owen bill was ruled unconstitutional. The courts said it interfered with labor agreements among private citizens.

Other moves to monitor child labor relied on social interactions rather than law. For example, street children who worked as newspaper sellers were joined as a group and overseen by groups like the National Newsboys' Association. This organization, which spread throughout the country in 200 branches, monitored working conditions and finances but also promoted upright behavior. By supporting its own community of newspaper sellers, the youths prepared themselves for living in a community as adults.

Mainly, those who worked at any job at a young age remembered the experience as their entry to the work world. They needed the money, sometimes lied about their ages to get work, and

The Triangle Shirtwaist Fire and After

On March 26, 1911, a fire at New York's Triangle Shirtwaist Company killed 146 workers. There was national grief at those lost, most of whom were young female Jewish or Italian immigrants. There was also outrage at the discovery that the deaths might have been prevented if the factory doors had been left open and fire escapes kept in working condition. The outrage led activists and politicians to take action and change public safety legislation for industrial workplaces. It also inched U.S. voters toward certain shifts in their political thinking.

In the weeks following the fire, newspapers like the *New York Times* investigated the event. They found that the factory owners had prevented employees from escaping. This brought heightened awareness of the lax safety rules in the garment industry. Ultimately it led to the passage of benchmark New York State laws governing workplace safety matters, such as heat monitoring and ventilation. It also led to improved conditions for female workers.

At the same time, the fire fueled some Americans' existing prejudice against big businesses. Because factory owners had bolted the door shut, many voters looked for representatives who were not connected to big business. Generally this meant Socialist candidates. In the 1910s, several cities elected Socialist politicians, including mayors in Berkeley, California, and Butte, Montana. Further, in the 1912 presidential election, the public turned away from traditionally business-oriented Republican candidates and elected a Democratic New Jersey governor named Woodrow Wilson.

The New York World newspaper reports the tragedy. (Library of Congress)

found the entry into an adult world exciting. One man recalled working part-time on a farm and with road teams when he was a teenager. At that time, he lied about his age and got a full-time job as a steelworker. One girl got started at her family's restaurant business even earlier, washing dishes at age five. "I'd get up on a Coca-Cola box to bend over the dish trough."

Harry McShane, child laborer who lost his arm in a Cincinnati, Ohio, spring factory accident; and an anonymous fourteen-year-old girl at an Adams, Massachusetts, textile mill. (Library of Congress)

Retirement and Pensions

Between 1900 and 1920, the life span of a U.S. resident increased by several years. What workers considered the end of their working years began to change during this time. The idea that people should stop working and spend part of their lives retired gained popularity.

In response, the number of older nonworking males over age sixty-five increased. In 1870, 25 percent of workers over age 65 were not actively working, but by 1920 the number had increased to 33 percent.

During this time, more Americans stopped working without pensions or retirement funds. The idea of retiring from a job and collecting a pension afterward from employers gained some popularity, but it was by no means widespread. The vast majority of companies offered no pensions. The few that did included transit corporations like the Baltimore and Ohio Railroad and craft unions like the United Brotherhood of Carpenters and Joiners. Yet they had limitations. Not only did the pensions pay only a small fraction of the person's wage, they were made available to only a small number of workers.

At the time, the U.S. government offered only one large-scale pension plan, which was to Civil War veterans. By 1920, the government had paid out $5 billion to Union soldiers.

Business and religious leaders dismissed the idea of a national old-age pension as unpatriotic and against the American concept of individuality. The U.S. government would not approve the national pension program known as Social Security in 1935.

The Workers' Long Road

In the first Labor Day parade in 1882, workers carried a sign asking for "Eight Hours of Work, Eight Hours of Rest, and Eight Hours for What We Will." In 1894, President Grover Cleveland made Labor Day official. He proclaimed it to celebrate the contributions of working people. The holiday was marked by workers' parades and plays championing union solidarity.

Yet despite gaining some protection through labor negotiations and government legislation, the eight-hour day was still a dream for most workers. Even at the Ford plant, considered a model, work was tough. The wife of an assembly-line worker wrote to Henry Ford in 1914, "That chain system you have is a slave driver!...Can't it be remedied?...That $5 a day is a blessing—a bigger one than you know but oh they earn it."

By 1920, the American worker still had a long way to go.

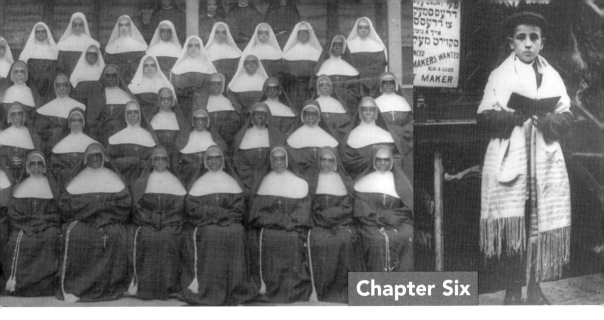

Chapter Six

Religion

During the early twentieth century, Americans practiced their religions in great numbers and in increasing variety. Nearly all Americans believed in God or a higher force. Most believers belonged to Protestant denominations such as the Baptists, Methodists, Presbyterians, and Disciples of Christ. However, millions of immigrants arrived from Ireland and southern Europe in the late nineteenth and early twentieth centuries. Most of them were Roman Catholics. By the start of the Great War, Roman Catholicism was the largest single U.S. denomination.

Catholics were only part of an increase in church attendance at the turn of the century. The twentieth century would also see an increase in religions in the United States. Among them were several varieties of Judaism. They were practiced by Jews who came from Germany in the nineteenth century and southern and eastern Europe in the late nineteenth and early twentieth centuries. Religions new to the United States, such as Hinduism, Buddhism, and Eastern Orthodox religions, were introduced.

Late nineteenth-century spiritual practices not linked to a traditional church also became popular. Among them were Christian Science, which emphasized spiritual healing, and "theosophy," a religious philosophy with mystical concerns.

By 1920, there were many threats to the variety of religious practices. Most immediate was prejudice. Some Americans dis-

Sisters of the Holy Family, in New Orleans, in about 1900 (LEFT). **A young Jewish boy in New York City** (RIGHT) **reads from a prayer book during Jewish New Year celebrations.** (Library of Congress)

trusted believers who did not look like them or did not share their religion. Because of this prejudice, Roman Catholics, Jews, and African American Protestants were often persecuted. Religious prejudice ranged from the anti-Semitism (against Jews) of American social leaders like Henry Ford and William Jennings Bryan to the organized assaults of the Ku Klux Klan. The Klan attacked Catholics, Jews, and African Americans.

Some challenges of the twentieth century came to all religions. The terror of world war, the speed of urban industrial life, and the acceptance of scientific thinking eroded belief in religion. Although more Americans worshipped regularly, they faced the problem of how to remain religious and yet live in a secular society. The problem came to a head in 1925 when a teacher named John Scopes was put on trial for teaching evolution.

Protestants in Power

At the turn of the century, there were many Protestant denominations in America. As society became more modern, they debated among themselves about what they believed and how they practiced their beliefs. A small, liberal group began to form around what it called the Social Gospel. But the majority of Protestants followed the beliefs of the evangelical, or conservative, denominations. They shared five basic core beliefs, which were the virgin birth of Jesus Christ, his physical resurrection after death, the holy accuracy of the Scriptures, salvation through atonement for one's sins and belief in Jesus, and believers' physical resurrection after his return to earth. These beliefs were discussed, collected, and published between 1909 and 1912 in twelve booklets called *The Fundamentals: A Testimony to the Truth*. They were funded and distributed by oil tycoons Lyman and Milton Stewart. The Stewarts said they wanted to distribute these booklets "to every pastor, evangelist, minister, theology professor, theological student, Sunday school super-

Christianity in the United States

The following table lists the number of adherents to selected Christian denominations, in millions of people.

DENOMINATION	1907	1917
Roman Catholicism	13.09	17.02
Selected Protestant Denominations:		
Presbyterian	1.30	1.58
Methodist	4.73	5.97
Southern Baptist	2.14	2.84

Source: Historical Statistics of the United States

The Social Gospel Movement: What Would Jesus Do?

"I view this world as a wrecked vessel," said the evangelical preacher Dwight Moody. He was not alone. Many early twentieth-century Protestant leaders thought industrial America could not be saved. Working and living conditions were too depraved. The most they could do was to save some individuals.

At the same time, other Protestant thinkers said that Christianity could and should reform society. They were followers of the belief system known as Christian Socialism. They preached what was known as the Social Gospel.

The movement arose in the 1870s as a way to use Christian principles to improve a troubled society. One of the movement's leaders was Walter Rauschenbusch. In 1907, he published a book called *Christianity and the Social Crisis*. He drew on his experiences as a Baptist minister in a poor New York City neighborhood called Hell's Kitchen. He said that Protestants who followed the Social Gospel could bring "spiritual health" to people and to society. They could make these changes by getting involved in politics and trying to reform workplaces. They would also need to work for long-range economic goals, like making the economic system fairer for the poor.

The hopeful Social Gospel had its critics. Mostly they were evangelical Protestants who found the Social Gospel's belief in human goodness unacceptable. Still, the Social Gospel inspired many reform actions. Among them were settlement houses and organizations like the Salvation Army. Among the Salvation Army's programs were homeless residences, children's night schools, and adult education classes.

Some Social Gospel clergymen wrote nonfiction books about how the United States might be changed. One of the most popular titles was Kansas minister Charles M. Sheldon's 1896 book *In His Steps*. Sheldon wondered what Jesus would think if He visited the United States. The book summarized Christian thinking in the question, "What would Jesus do?" *In His Steps* was a best-seller for sixty years and sold 8 million copies.

Followers of the Social Gospel also discussed some of the weightiest problems of the era. During World War I, they accused Germany of a broader evil that they claimed was the reason behind U.S. involvement in the conflict. In a 1917 editorial in *Christian Century* called "The War and the Social Gospel," editors said, "The sin we are fighting is not of the individual German soldier through whose breasts our boys have to run their bayonets, but the social sin of the German nation as a whole."

The Social Gospel's questions about good, evil, and social justice remained relevant for decades. Many of its followers' goals were realized by organized labor and the New Deal that would follow the Great Depression. In the mid-twentieth century, they inspired another minister who thought society could be transformed— the Reverend Martin Luther King, Jr.

intendent, YMCA and YWCA [Young Men's and Young Women's Christian Associations] secretary in the English-speaking world."

Throughout the 1910s, preachers of small and large revival meetings praised Biblical literalism. These preachers believed that every idea in the Bible was absolute fact. To show unity and recruit new members, some Protestant churches formed an unofficial coalition to spread Protestant practices. These practices included Sunday school, home prayer, bible study, and camp meetings.

Camp meetings allowed evangelical Protestants to demonstrate their faith. They were held outdoors and often had audiences of hundreds or thousands. At these meetings, a preacher would deliver sermons on basic Christian beliefs and the terrible consequences of not following them. Those who were not Christian were urged to confess their sins and convert.

Sometimes these meetings were led by an energetic traveling preacher called a revivalist. Among the best-known revivalists was Dwight Moody, founder of the Moody Bible Institute in Chicago. Moody preached a conservative set of beliefs called "Old Fashion Gospel." He spoke plainly and in simple language. But in the early twentieth century, he was surpassed in popularity by the former baseball player and orphan turned evangelist William "Billy" Sunday.

Billy Sunday remade the camp meeting. It became longer and more sophisticated. On Sundays, the meetings moved into tents and churchlike areas called tabernacles. The tabernacles could hold a larger group. Before the meeting started, there were marching bands, choirs, and other entertainment. Sunday also made the preaching itself more entertaining. He peppered his reli-

This wide-angle photograph taken during one of Billy Sunday's Tabernacle meetings shows how large the crowds were when the famous preacher came to town. (Library of Congress)

gious beliefs with slang and high emotion.

In the early twentieth century, millions of people saw and heard Billy Sunday. In many ways, Sunday represented popular thinking on American issues. For example, he was a staunch supporter of U.S. involvement in the Great War, once troops were sent abroad. He promoted patriotism at his revivals, saying, "Christianity and patriotism are synonymous terms, and hell and traitors are synonymous."

Protestants taught their beliefs to their children and new members in Sunday school. The programs were highly organized and differed among denominations. But all were considered central to bringing in and training new members. Teachers often belonged to larger, nationally organized groups that provided training and monitored the number of new members. These groups included the "Baraca" for men and the "Philathea" for women. Because Sunday school could bring in new members, it was often considered more important than other church activities.

Another reason for Protestantism's popularity was that it appealed to the rich and influential. Besides hundreds of thousands of average citizens, most of the nation's business leaders chose Protestantism. For example, major early twentieth-century business leaders such as oil tycoon John D. Rockefeller and banker J. P. Morgan belonged to Protestant churches. For his Baptist church, Rockefeller helped

Billy Sunday (Library of Congress)

A Catholic church in Leopold, Missouri. (Library of Congress)

run Sunday school and donated hundreds of millions of dollars. Morgan gave millions of dollars to his Episcopal church and invited its bishops to discuss world affairs. Episcopalians (the U.S. branch of the Church of England) attracted more multimillionaires than any other. Half of New York City's seventy-five multimillionaires belonged to the Episcopal church. The Protestant ethic of hard work represented a seriousness and thriftiness that suited businessmen.

Catholics Gain Strength

Protestant denominations accounted for more Americans than any other religion. But Roman Catholics made up the largest single religious group. They increased from over 6.2 million in 1880 to over 19.8 million in 1920. In 1908, Pope Pius X said that the United States was no longer a missionary territory. This meant that it did not have to import clergy or other forms of aid from other countries. There were enough American Catholics to support the religion and even to send missionaries to other countries.

The Roman Catholic Church in America had already developed its own image. In 1908, Chicago Archbishop William H. O'Connell said that it had already "taken on a character of its own; become conscious of its own mission and destiny; and . . . is prepared to go forth conquering and to conquer in the cause of Christ."

Generally Catholics did not debate differences in their aims or community purpose. Instead they marked differences through the ethnic flavor of their parishes. Many parishes represented the southern and eastern European countries from which their people came, like Italy, Slovakia, and Poland. They decorated their churches with the home country's saints or other religious ethnic art. These parishes added to the already numerous Irish- and German-influenced Catholic churches. All services, however, were conducted in Latin.

In the early part of the century, Catholicism also attracted

African Americans. They may have been introduced to the religion in Catholic school or liked the church's aim to include all people. An all–African American and Native American order of nuns began in 1891, and an all–African American seminary for priests opened in 1920.

Although some parishes appealed to the Vatican to establish separate ethnic churches, the Vatican did not approve their request. American church leaders disapproved of this as well. In 1891, Baltimore's James Cardinal Gibbons called for unity among Catholics of varied European origins. He asked them to "glory in the title of American citizen."

In nearly all Catholic parishes, church social organizations were important to keeping the church unified. Among these organizations were sodalities (for women) and youth groups. Even more important was the Catholic school. It added funds to the parish and brought converts into the religion. American churches started building schools in large numbers after they were directed to do so by the church's Third Plenary Council in 1884. By 1920, there were many dozens of Catholic schools. In addition to conveying Roman Catholicism to future generations, parochial schools also attracted students of other religions. The students were brought by parents who did not wish to send their children to public schools.

The Jewish Population Grows

Jews had been in North America for 300 years, but they increased substantially during the mid-nineteenth and early twentieth centuries. Unlike their predecessors, the new Jewish immigrants set up a distinct religious and social existence.

In the mid-nineteenth century, about 250,000 German and other European Jews immigrated to the United States. They fitted themselves into the largely Protestant American culture. While

This turn-of-the-century poster advertises free English classes for newly arrived Jewish immigrants. (Library of Congress)

they attended synagogues, they did not build yeshivas (schools) for their children's education. Instead they sent their children to public schools.

However, the 2 million Jews who came later built their own religious and cultural communities. They established synagogues, yeshivas (or religious schools), mutual-aid groups, and Yiddish entertainment. (Yiddish is a German-based language spoken by Jews originally in Eastern Europe.) In these communities, many Jews practiced a more traditional version of their religion than earlier immigrants. Many were Orthodox, or strictly religious, Jews, and some attended prayer services every day.

By the 1920s, Jews had established several national organizations to unite Jews and make their religion better known. In 1926, the Synagogue Council of America brought the various types of Judaism together. The Society for Advancement of Judaism kept the religion active.

While Jews built up their religion, the Ku Klux Klan and other anti-Jewish groups worked against them. To the Klan, fighting the Jewish religion was noble. It helped maintain a Protestant America. As KKK Wizard Hiram Wesley Evans said, "Protestantism is an essential part of Americanism; without it, America would never have been created and without it she cannot go forward." Among the many attacks on Jews during the period was the lynching in Georgia of Jewish factory owner Leo Frank in 1913. Frank was wrongly accused of murdering a little girl, but he was taken from jail and hung by a mob.

African American Churches

Since the late 1700s, African Americans had operated their own Protestant churches. Many were of Baptist and Methodist denominations because those churches allowed blacks to be trained as preachers. After the Civil War and into the early twentieth century, African Americans established and worshipped in even more independent Christian churches. By 1900, about 3 million African Americans belonged to a church, most of them in black denominations.

Popular denominations included the African Methodist Episcopal (AME) church, which had been a force in the North during the nineteenth century. One of its leaders was Daniel Alexander Payne. He founded churches in denominations

Women's groups like the Women's National Baptist Convention provided food, clothing, housing assistance, and educational opportunities for poor African Americans.
(Library of Congress)

including AME and the Colored Cumberland Presbyterians. Other churches, like the Colored Methodist Episcopal Church, were founded by former slaves. Membership grew steadily among all these churches. By 1920, about 40 percent of African Americans were church members.

Because they wanted to worship in different ways, some African American Protestants looked for a different kind of church. They wanted to experience the Holy Spirit in a more direct and intense way. This search for holiness led to the founding of the Church of God in Christ. The church was founded in 1897 by Charles Mason and Charles Jones. One gift of the spirit practiced in the church was speaking in tongues. This was a holy but untranslatable spiritual language. In 1907, the church founders disagreed about speaking in tongues, and split up. The Church of God in Christ remained the leading Pentecostal church for African Americans.

Because they were usually the only local black institution, African American churches were especially important to the community. In 1903, cultural leader W. E. B. Du Bois called African

Marcus Garvey, founder of the Universal Negro Improvement Association, preached a style of Christianity aimed especially at blacks.
(Library of Congress)

American churches "the social center of Negro life in the United States." He said they were a "social, intellectual, and economic center" as well as a religious one.

Between 1870 and 1930, 2.5 million African Americans moved out of the South. Nearly half of them moved to cities. African Americans often set up new churches when they immigrated. In many ways, urban religious life differed from rural worship. One difference was scale. Urban churches were usually much larger than rural ones. They served a larger and more diverse congregation. A rural church might have dozens of members. A big city church might have several thousand members and a web of social services like schools and employment centers.

Other African American religious associations and activities also formed. Among them was the National Baptist Convention. The organization stayed important even after it split into two parts in 1907. The newly formed groups included the National Baptist Convention of America and the National Baptist Convention of the U.S.A., Inc.

Other spiritual leaders shaped African American beliefs. In the 1910s, Jamaican-born Marcus Garvey organized African Americans to work for a movement called Pan-Africanism. The movement encouraged black pride and the sharing of common goals. To promote those ideas and the idea that people of African ancestry worldwide should return to African to claim it as their homeland, Garvey founded the Universal Negro Improvement Association (UNIA) in 1914.

With the slogan "One God, One Aim, One Destiny," UNIA attracted thousands of Africans in the United States and across the world. UNIA presented a Christianity especially for blacks, and in 1921 produced The Universal Negro Catechism. The movement remained strong until Garvey was convicted of mail fraud in the mid-1920s and was deported.

Other Practices

Although the Nation of Islam did not start until the 1930s, another order of black American Muslims began in 1913. It was called Moorish Science and was founded by Noble Drew Ali. The group worshiped at the Moorish Science Temple in Newark, New Jersey. Its beliefs came from a text called "The Holy Koran," which was different from the ancient Koran. Moorish Science called for blacks to reclaim their heritage as Moroccans. (Morocco is a Muslim country in North Africa.)

Other groups were distinctly American as well. Among them was the Church of Christ (Scientist). It had been founded in 1875 by American spiritualist Mary Baker Eddy. In her guidebook *Science and Health According to the Scriptures* (1875), she focused on spirituality, not a deity. Among her most controversial beliefs was that the human body could be healed through prayer and a strong belief in God. In 1898, the Christian Science movement set up the Christian Science Publishing Company to promote the religion worldwide. In 1908, it founded a newspaper, *The Christian Science Monitor*.

The 1893 World's Parliament of Religions in Chicago had introduced major non-Christian religions. Speakers discussed Hinduism, Buddhism, and Islam. Following the meeting, groups

The First Church of Christian Science in Boston, Massachusetts. (Library of Congress)

The Morman Temple in Salt Lake City, Utah, in 1912. (Library of Congress)

formed to promote those religions. In 1900, the Young Men's Buddhist Association was founded. Other practitioners of these religions started arriving from Asia.

The Mormons, who belonged to the Church of Jesus Christ of Latter-Day Saints, increased their numbers during the period. In 1870, the Mormon population was about 140,000. By 1916, it was 450,000.

Many Orthodox Christian churches increased their numbers because of immigration. Among the biggest and most powerful were the Greek and Russian Orthodox churches. There were many Orthodox churches, one for each ethnic group, like Serbians and Arabs. Unlike the Roman Catholic church, the Orthodox churches did not band together in an organized diocese (administration). The lack of unity in Orthodox churches limited their national power. As Greek Orthodox Archbishop Platon reported in the early twentieth century, "Although the idea of a united leadership is so really important for the success of Orthodoxy in America . . . it seems it is not feasible. . . . "

Other less-common Christian religions also developed during the early twentieth century. The Church of the Seventh-Day Adventists grew from nearly 62,000 to more than 110,000 during the period. Jehovah's Witnesses increased to 15,000.

Urban Churches

The move from a rural to an urban way of life changed American religion profoundly. In some ways, the variety of people in the cities helped members grow stronger in their faiths. It also helped them become more tolerant of other religions. If churches, synagogues, and temples stood within a few blocks, it became easier to accept religious differences. But the mix of religions made other people feel uncomfortable. It also caused some people to lessen their ties to religion.

Another way the secular world competed with religion was in presenting scientific findings. Some people thought science and religion did not have to be enemies, but many conflicts developed between the two. Believers in science said their approach used testing and historical evidence to prove its findings. Religion, they said, could not prove its claims. Believers in religion said the believers in science were going too far. Some Christians believed that the Biblical story of creation was true in every detail. They said God had made each kind of living thing from nothing. They refused to accept the view of naturalist Charles Darwin that living things evolved from simpler forms. They were especially opposed to Darwin's theory that humans evolved from lower animals.

Religion and Modern Science

Charles Darwin's 1859 book *Origin of Species* caused conflict among Protestants. Many fundamentalist denominations thought Darwin's ideas on evolution went against the Bible. More liberal denominations thought there could be some agreement between Darwin and the Bible. By the end of the nineteenth century, the debate slowed. But as fundamentalist Protestantism became more popular in the early twentieth century, the uproar started again.

The debate between Darwinists and anti-Darwinists came to a head in the 1920s. At that time, a Tennessee public school-teacher named John Scopes was put on trial for teaching the scientific theories of evolution in his class. Scopes was challenged for presenting a non-Biblical view of creation. The trial ended with him being convicted. More than that, it showed a major twentieth-century tension between modern scientific thinking and long-held religious beliefs. The conflict between the two forces would continue in different ways into the twenty-first century.

Chapter Seven

Health, Science, and Technology

Chicago "Milk Ladies" (LEFT) **promote the importance of milk for children. Orville Wright** (RIGHT) **and his sister Katherine on board one of the Wright brothers' early airplanes. In 1903, Wright and his brother Wilbur became the first to successfully fly a piloted airplane.** (Library of Congress)

The early twentieth century was marked by major medical, scientific, and technological advances. For example, good nutrition helped people to live longer. Through scientific studies of food and vitamins, nutritionists learned about the qualities of specific foods. Even though more prepackaged and less nutritious foods were becoming popular, Americans also bought more healthful foods like fruit and milk.

Transportation expanded from the railroad and horse-drawn carriage to the airplane, automobile, subway, and electric trolley. With the mass-produced Model T, most Americans could afford to buy a car. By 1920, eight million were on the U.S. market. The Wright brothers successfully flew heavier-than-air airplanes and introduced them to the U.S. public through the military. They were crucial to World War I air fights.

The home was also transformed by electricity and new forms of communication. As more places were wired for electricity, inventors created more items to use it. Among them were vacuum cleaners, washing machines, and refrigerators. All made everyday chores easier. There was also the telephone, which was in many American homes by 1920. Finally, there was the radio. The first nationally aired program was broadcast in 1920.

Doctors, Nurses, and Hospitals

As scientists made new discoveries, the doctor, nurse, and hospital became accepted parts of American life. Doctors and nurses solidified their professions. Due to late nineteenth-century breakthroughs in the understanding of how diseases were spread, doctors were able to treat patients more effecively. They were trained professionals who used the latest medicines and surgical techniques to treat patients. Doctors belonged to professional groups like the American Medical Association and had to pass tests by licensing boards to be accredited. In 1911, nurses founded the American Nurses' Association to represent their interests.

Medical schools became more rigorous. These educational changes began in the late nineteenth century, through reformers at Harvard and Johns Hopkins medical schools. In 1909, a high school principal, Andrew Flexner, was hired by the Carnegie Foundation, the American Medical Association, and others to study medical school curricula and recommend reforms. Flexner was the brother of a physician and an expert on curricula. In the *Carnegie Bulletin Number Four*, he suggested that medical schools standardize and reorganize the curricula around laboratory science and clinical experience, as well as lectures. The report was modified by medical educators and other doctors. Unfortunately, it recommended excluding women, African Americans, and the poor from medical practice. By the early twentieth century, most medical schools adopted these recommendations. Where there had been twenty-six schools teaching women and/or African American doctors, only four remained. The image of a modern doctor was now an educated, well-to-do, white male.

In hospitals, doctors offered treatment that could not be carried out at home. They used specialized equipment, such as X-ray machines, for diagnosis. They treated patients with drugs like opiate (an opium-based narcotic) for pain and nitroglycerin to stimulate the heart. They used anesthesia to perform surgery.

Diseases and Epidemics

Infectious diseases were the most common causes of adult death in the early twentieth century. Often passed in epidemics that swept through towns and cities, they included influenza, tuberculosis, diphtheria, and polio. Each disease could be transmitted easily among humans. Each was common in industrialized areas with large populations. Tuberculosis and Spanish influenza caused the most massive loss of life over a short term in the United States.

When infectious diseases spread beyond national boundaries, they were called pandemics. The Spanish influenza pandemic of 1918 and 1919 killed over 20 million people worldwide and 550,000 Americans. It was the nation's most deadly epidemic to date. The disease was first identified in Kansas, with symptoms that included upset stomach, fever, nausea, and dizziness. Death often followed. The disease was unusual because it struck healthy adults rather than the elderly or young. It was passed by casual human contact, and did not have a cure. The epidemic ended when the virus affected as many people as it would by normal exposure, or when the virus mutated into another form. However, the power of the virus led scientists to do extensive viral research over the next decades.

Tuberculosis was called consumption, TB, or the "white plague." In 1900, it was the second greatest cause of death in the nation. That year, one out of every 500 Americans died from the disease. This bacterial lung infection spread quickly through terrible-sounding coughs, and there were no drugs to cure it. It was often fatal, but living amidst clean air could lessen symptoms. For that reason, more rural states such as Colorado and New Mexico became recovery sites for TB patients. Even so, in 1918, more than one out of every 660 Americans still died from tuberculosis.

In 1900, diphtheria killed about one out of every 2,300 Americans. Due to the discovery of a diphtheria antitoxin around 1900 and the development of a test that could tell doctors who was most likely to get the disease, the death rate was lowered to about one in every 6,800 Americans by 1922.

In 1916, a polio epidemic occurred, killing 6,000 of the more than 28,000 it affected. One of its lasting effects was paralysis. Future President Franklin Roosevelt was one of its victims in 1921. More serious polio epidemics would take place in the mid-twentieth century. Vaccines were not created until 1954.

Cancer was a deadly diagnosis during this era. Nine of ten Americans diagnosed with cancer died from the disease. And one out of every 1,500 Americans died from cancer. Unlike other serious diseases of the era, cancer was not contagious. While anti-toxins and vaccines controlled many infectious diseases, the number of people dying of cancer increased throughout the twentieth century.

A person's age and where they lived also had an effect on health. In the rural South, malaria could still be found. Carried by a mosquito in the summer, it infected the blood and led to high fevers. The disfiguring disease of rickets struck children who did not get enough vitamin D from diet or sunlight. By the 1920s, enriched dairy products and bread nearly ended the disease in the United States.

Despite medical advances, some old-fashioned home treatments continued. For example, the practice of bleeding was still used in some immigrant families to treat life-threatening diseases like pneumonia. Cupping, in which blood was drawn to the body's surface by heating a glass cup, and sweating out diseases were also practiced.

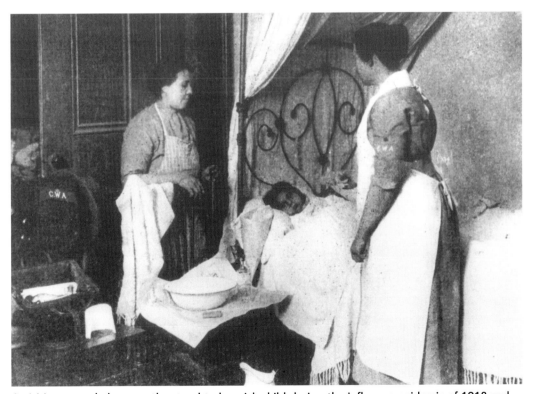

A visiting nurse helps a mother tend to her sick child during the influenza epidemic of 1918 and 1919. More than half a million Americans, and 20 million worldwide, died of the disease during that time. (National Library of Medicine)

The Medicine Cabinet

When early twentieth-century Americans became ill, they didn't immediately call the doctor. They often tried to cure themselves with something from their kitchen or medicine cabinet.

Home remedies like mustard plasters were common. Baking soda and water cured an upset stomach. Prunes, sauerkraut, or bran ended constipation. Salt was used to brush teeth before toothpaste became popular.

The medicine chest contained a mix of scientific advances, marvels of mass marketing, patent medicines, and old-fashioned home treatments. Among health notions were enemas, mouth gargles, and hand lotions. By the 1910s, antiperspirants became popular as part of daily hygiene and were added to the medicine cabinet. Medical equipment included trusses to support body parts and vibrators for massages.

One popular medicine was belladonna, an opiate used for heart problems and various types of pain. Castor oil was used to cure constipation.

Some patent medicines had fatal side effects. In a 1905 exposé, *Collier's* magazine reported that a child in Cincinnati died from an overdose of opium after "drinking the contents of a bottle of Doctor Bull's Cough Syrup." It and the *Ladies' Home Journal* also reported on how the patent medicine companies misrepresented the products and avoided lawsuits. The magazines called the patent medicine companies "the poison trusts." In 1906, the Pure Food and Drug Act regulated patent medicines and other drugs. (See Chapter 3.)

Perhaps the most popular medication in the cabinet was acetylsalicylic acid. Unlike opiate, it was not addictive. This pain reliever was created by chemists in Germany, who held the rights to the drug. It was originally packaged in powder form, but it became more popular among Americans when it came in tablet form in 1915. The drug was so popular throughout the world that it became part of the Treaty of Versailles at the end of World War I. As part of its payment to the victors, Germany (which lost the war) had to deliver the rights to the drug. It became the simple over-the-counter drug it is today, aspirin.

Many of the non-prescription or patent medicines sold in the early twentieth century did little to cure illness. Others were downright dangerous. This issue of *Collier's* magazine exposed some of the most dangerous medicines for sale and led the government to pass new safety laws. (Library of Congress)

Sanitation, Nutrition, and Public Health

Several public health practices helped to increase the life span of the average American. Better sanitation was important to improving public health. Cities began to see public health as one of their civic responsibilities. By the mid-1910s, most cities and towns collected garbage regularly and used street cleaning machines to remove trash and rats, and fleas and mosquitoes that fed on them. When scientific findings showed that tuberculosis and other diseases could be spread by germs, local and state governments replaced the water buckets in train stations where people drank from a shared dipper. This change led to the development of the paper Dixie cup, for individual use.

Many people tried to make their homes more hygienic. Fearing epidemics, they cleaned with disinfectants, bathed and washed more frequently, and removed visible dirt. This move toward cleanliness was supported in government writings and in advertisements. The government writings linked cleanliness to good citizenship. Meanwhile, advertisements linked it to a high social class.

Improved nutrition also increased the American life span.

Most American cities were far dirtier than they are today. Rats were a common sight. By the turn of the twentieth century, however, more attention was paid to sanitation. For example, Philadelphia's Department of Health operated a "rat patrol" to capture and exterminate the disease-carrying rodents. (National Library of Medicine)

Nutritionists such as Elmer McCollum presented studies that showed the poor health effects of vitamin deficiencies. For example, he showed that an absence of vitamin B could bring on the disease beri beri. Beri beri weakens the muscles and often leads to paralysis and death. That and other nutrition information was popularized for newspapers and women's magazines such as the *Ladies' Home Journal*.

By the late 1910s, the ideal of a healthy body changed. Stout men and fleshy women were no longer ideals. Instead, government health experts and the press promoted a lean image. Experts recommended a diet with lower levels of protein, higher levels of vitamins C and D, and fewer calories. Doctors recommended slimming down, and images of movie stars and sports figures popularized it. Even 350-pound President William Howard Taft lost dozens of pounds to appear healthier for an election campaign.

Railroads, Streetcars, and Subways

At the turn of the twentieth century, the horse-drawn vehicle was becoming a relic of the past.

Beginning in the 1870s, U.S. railroads had spread to big city terminals and small-town commuter stops. Transcontinental rail service began in the 1890s and became popular for business and personal use. By the turn of the century, railroads were the largest U.S. industry. They employed 1.7 million workers and bought more coal, iron, and steel than any other business. By 1920, there were more railroad tracks in the U.S. than in any other country. Trains bought people together and transported consumer goods more quickly than ever before. A train left Chicago every four minutes. The 1915 Twentieth Century Limited traveled between New York and Chicago in twenty hours.

There were other rail innovations. Since the late 1880s, the electric streetcar, or trolley, had transformed city travel. These vehicles pulled by overhead cables gained popularity. By 1900, there were 30,000 streetcars owned by about 1,000 different streetcar lines and running on 15,000 miles of track. Trolleys ran at speeds of up to 20 miles per hour and were so efficient that their fares declined from ten cents to five cents. In 1917, trolley ridership reached its peak at 11 billion riders along 45,000 miles of track.

Cities also had other types of elevated and underground railways. They were useful in difficult areas, like steep hills, and in highly populated areas. Aboveground railways included Chicago's els, or elevated lines. Subways ran up long avenues and under bodies of water in Boston (1897) and New York (1904).

Everywhere, transportation was improving. U.S. engineer John Phillip Holland designed the first modern submarine for the U.S. Navy in 1900. Benjamin Holt invented the tractor in 1901.

The Airplane

Since the late 1800s, American inventors were trying to build a machine that would permit humans to fly in the air. In 1893 on Lake Michigan, inventor Hiram Maxim tested a steam-powered flying machine that could carry a crew, but it crashed. In Virginia in 1896, Smithsonian Institution secretary Samuel Langley flew a machine powered by a steam engine for 3,000 feet. He adapted the machine to carry a pilot, but failed to launch it in September 1903.

At around the same time, Ohio bicycle shop owners Orville and Wilbur Wright were test-flying motorized gliders. Through tests over three years, they improved their machine's ability to hover and be guided. They refined the engine placement and the wings' ability to be maneuvered. On December 17, 1903, in Kitty Hawk, North Carolina, they tested the machine. It flew, with pilot, for twelve seconds. In later tests, it flew for about a minute.

In 1910, the Wrights demonstrated their flying machine for the U.S. armed forces. They signed a contract, and with the

The first airplane takes to the skies at Kitty Hawk, North Carolina, in 1903. Orville Wright lies flat on an engine-powered glider as his brother Wilbur runs alongside. In that first flight, the plane flew for twelve seconds. (Library of Congress)

improvements designed by mechanical innovator Glenn Curtiss, they produced airplanes for the military. These airplanes were used successfully for air battles, or dogfights, in Europe. The airplane captured the American public's imagination. In the 1920s, it would begin to become part of civilian life.

The Automobile

In the late nineteenth century, Americans had experimented with an engine-driven road vehicle. The Duryea brothers were the first to make more than one of the same vehicle. They fought a cultural battle with horse lovers, who thought the horse was more natural and more dependable than a car. But designer J. Frank Duryea replied "the horse is a willful, unreliable brute…. The mechanical motor is his superior in many respects." By 1899, more than 20 U.S. companies produced over 2,500 cars.

Most of the early vehicles were electrical or steam powered. But the practical motor vehicle of the twentieth century was gasoline-driven. Michigan inventor Ransom Olds developed a one-cylinder two-seater. He aimed to make beautiful vehicles, no matter what their cost. Michigan mechanic Henry Ford, on the other hand, aimed to build a "universal car" that most people could afford. His Ford Motor Company made its first vehicle in 1903. The Model T was Ford's $850 "motor car for the great multitude." In 1909 and 1910, he produced over 18,000 cars at $950 each. By 1920 and 1921, he sold 1,250,000 cars.

By 1910, cars had become so popular that one designer said, "The novelty of owning an automobile has largely worn off. The neighbors have one of their own." By 1912, there were nearly 950,000 autos registered in the U.S. By 1920, the United States had become a nation of automobiles. More than 8 million passenger cars were registered, and hundreds of thousands of Americans made their livings by producing, selling, or servicing cars. Millions more had jobs tied to the automobile, such as hotel, restaurant, and resort owners. Town planners had to widen and pave roads to fit cars.

Yet as much as the car changed the economy and the layout of communities, it also changed the way people felt about travel. It made travel more personalized and self-controlled. As *Motor Car* magazine said, "You are your master….Time and space at your beck and call; your freedom is complete."

Henry Ford (LEFT), creator of the Model T, made owning a car affordable for average Americans. He is seen here with the great inventor Thomas Edison, who had invented the phono-graph, or record player, in 1877 and the lightbulb in 1879.
(Library of Congress)

The Electrical Age

After Thomas Alva Edison demonstrated the incandescent bulb in 1879, electricity became a source of household energy. Its popularity grew quickly. In 1907, 8 percent of U.S. households had electrical service. That percentage had doubled to 16 by 1912 and reached 35 by 1920.

Most people continued to have gas-fueled furnaces and stoves. But they used electricity for lighting. Customers got gas and electricity from organizations called utilities that controlled these power sources. These utilities generated customers by show-ing how easy the new energy sources were for consumers. Once customers had gas and electrical service, they did not have to buy kerosene lamps or candles. The power source was always there.

Adding to the popularity of electricity was its lower price. By the 1920s, electricity became much cheaper than it had been 30 years earlier. Many more sources of electricity were harnessed by building dams on huge waterways like Niagara Falls in New York.

Utilities interested people in using more electricity by selling electrical appliances. Some of them offered free trials of irons and other appliances. If customers liked the appliances, they could buy them. By the mid-1910s, many upper- and middle-class U.S. homes had electric appliances. Most were designed for the kitchen, like the coffee pot, electric mixer, and toaster. Others made housekeeping simpler, like the washing machine, sewing machine, vacuum cleaner, and electric iron. Electric refrigerators were available by 1920. They were advertised in newspapers and women's magazines. Because fewer homes had servants to do housework, the new appliances were advertised as "mechanical servants." But most working class and some rural households did not have electrical service or appliances until the 1930s and 1940s. Even in 1940, only 35 percent of those in rural areas had electricity.

The Telephone

In the late nineteenth century, inventor Alexander Graham Bell presented his telephone at the Philadelphia Centennial Exhibition. By the turn of the century, there were over one million telephones in U.S. homes. Service kept improving. By 1915, people could make transcontinental phone calls. By 1920, Bell or other experimenters like Missouri inventor Almon Strowger had refined the telephone. It changed from its original box design to a more streamlined candlestick shape. The automatic switchboard allowed many calls to be processed at the same time.

Early telephones featured bells that were cranked by hand. Just as they do today, telephones worked by converting sound to electrical impulses and then back to sound.
(Library of Congress)

By 1920, there were 13.3 million phones. In all its forms, the telephone was a common part of the office and home. As British social critic Arnold Bennett observed, "The American telephone conveyed the voice with such speed and clarity that it invited the most intimate reflections....You can see [a woman] at morn at her bedroom window, pouring confidences into her telephone."

Entertainment Technology

The phonograph, which reproduced sound, was first demonstrated in 1877 by Thomas Alva Edison. The machine was a metal cylinder that had grooves and could record sounds onto a sheet of foil and play them back. Edison patented the device and formed the Edison Speaking Phonograph Company. Then he turned his attention to another of his inventions, the incandescent light bulb.

By the turn of the century, many Americans had phonographs with wax cylinders in their homes. Then, in 1896, German immigrant Emile Berliner advanced technology further. Instead of using cylinders, he developed flat master plates. From them, large numbers of copies could be made and sold. The flat discs were called records.

In 1921, over 100 million phonographs were made. The early boom in recorded music purchases also soared, reaching its peak in 1920. Afterward, sales declined because of another technological invention, the radio.

Radio was developed in the 1890s by Italian engineer Guglielmo Marconi. Many engineers tried to refine radio for wide use, including American engineer Lee DeForest. He developed many inventions for the radio, including the vacuum tube and a microphone. In 1916, he broadcast the first radio news report.

Starting in 1893, George Eastman advertised his cameras using young women that were known as "Kodak Girls." (Library of Congress)

Four years later, in 1920, the world's first radio station began broadcasting. It was KDKA in Pittsburgh, and it reported on the presidential election of Republican candidate Warren Harding. During the 1920s, radio would change the way Americans got their news and entertainment.

Another product that enhanced everyday life was the personal Kodak camera. Professional documentary makers and artists had taken photographs in the 1800s. Late in the century, inventor George Eastman made them for the general public. By 1900, 100,000 Kodak cameras were in use by amateurs. That year, a designer for Eastman created a new camera that made photography easier. It was an inexpensive one-dollar camera for children called the Brownie. It was advertised by tiny elf-like characters called brownies. Adults liked the Brownie, too. It became the standard family camera. Photographs increased and photography became more informal.

American Science Changes

Most American scientists of nineteenth and early twentieth centuries were interested in applied science, or technology. They worked to solve everyday problems. There were many such

American scientist-innovators as the Wright brothers with their airplanes, Bell with his telephone, and Edison with his many practical inventions such as the light bulb, the phonograph, and many improvements on the telegraph, telephone, and motion pictures.

Many of the ideas that would shape future twentieth-century American science came from Europe. In 1505, the German scientist Albert Einstein published a number of breakthrough theories dealing with time, light, energy, and matter. Einstein's theories challenged ideas that had governed the study of physics since the seventeenth century. Two of the most important were that space and time are not absolute and that light can be both wave and particle. A third was summed up in the formula $E=mc^2$. In other words, the energy of a body is equal to its mass times the speed of light squared. At first, Einstein's theories seemed to have little practical application. Over time, however, they caused revolutionary uses of the atom and greatly contributed to understanding of the universe.

In 1901, the John D. Rockefeller and Andrew Carnegie families endowed institutes for scientific research. As the twentieth century progressed, Americans began to focus on pure laboratory science. The outcome of these scientists' experiments in biology, chemistry, and physics could not quickly be put to practical use, so institutional support was key to their work.

Scientists also took great interest in astronomy. Percival Lowell set up an observatory in Arizona in 1894, where he first studied the planet Mars. The astronomer Charles Perrine found the sixth and seventh satellites of the most distant known planet, Neptune. Lowell became convinced that there was a planet beyond Neptune,

Darwin and Freud

Two Europeans who were neither inventors nor laboratory scientists influenced scientific thought greatly in the twentieth century.

The Englishman Charles Darwin had written his *Origin of Species by Means of Natural Selection* in 1859. His suggestion that all life, including that of humans, evolved over time from simpler forms created a religious backlash in the United States. (See Chapter 6.)

In 1899, the Austrian Dr. Sigmund Freud published *The Interpretation of Dreams*. Freud was a neurologist who treated patients in Vienna by letting them tell him their thoughts while relaxing on a couch. He introduced the ideas that people have unconscious motives, and that children have sexual feelings. Freud presented these and other ideas at a series of 1909 lectures at Clark University in Worchester, Massachusetts. In time, he would have a large following in the United States.

Sigmund Freud
(Library of Congress)

which he called X. (The planet Pluto would not be discovered until after he died.) Meanwhile, at Harvard, Henrietta Swan Leavitt studied the varying magnitude, or brightness, of stars. She determined in 1908 that these variables could be used to measure their distances from Earth. Back at the Lowell Observatory, Vesto Melvin Slipher studied nebulas, bodies of gas or dust in space. In 1912, he was able to measure how fast they moved.

Other scientists were interested in advancing biology. In 1901, Walter Sutton published a paper on how chromosomes carry hereditary factors. Thomas Hunt Morgan began to study the genes of fruit flies at Columbia University. Working with others, he determined that genes are linked in pairs on chromosomes and responsible for specific traits passed from one generation to the next. Although his work was published in 1916, Morgan did not win the Nobel Prize in Physiology or Medicine until 1933. Only two Americans won the Nobel during the era. Albert Michaelson won in physics in 1907 for precise measurement of the speed of light. Theodore Richards won in chemistry in 1914 for determining the atomic weight of twenty-five elements.

World War I had helped focus scientific efforts in aviation. In 1915, the National Advisory Committee for Aeronautics was set up. It would become in 1958 the National Aeronautics and Space Administration. American science was now set on a new course. Its scientists were beginning to compete with those in Europe on more equal ground. Later in the century, they would set the pace.

Leisure, Sports, and Entertainment

Native American athlete Jim Thorpe (LEFT) **was considered by many the greatest American athlete of all time. Not only did he play football for the Carlisle Indian School in Pennsylvania, but he played nine other sports as well and won two Olympic Gold Medals. Ringling Brothers-Barnum and Bailey Circus has entertained all ages since its founding in 1871. This poster** (RIGHT) **is from 1911.** (Library of Congress)

In the early twentieth century, Americans worked fewer hours than they had a century ago and had more time to themselves. Social critics like Thorstein Veblen called this free time leisure. This leisure was limited. An office worker might have two days off per week, while a laborer had one day. Some had only partial days. Middle- and upper-class people took vacations, but paid vacation was rare among the working class.

Despite these limitations, there were plenty of sports and entertainment to fill people's free time. Some, like playing amateur sports and going to public parks, were free. Professional sports, vaudeville, and the movies were businesses. To enjoy them cost money. Less costly was the popular pursuit of reading—newspapers, magazines, and popular fiction.

Because more Americans than ever lived in towns and cities, many leisure activities were aimed at a large audience. Professional baseball games were played in a stadium like Brooklyn's Ebbets Field, which seated tens of thousands of people. Seats came in a variety of prices, just as they did in vaudeville halls and theaters.

While the twentieth century had many leisure activities that brought people together, some amusements were more passive and private. While a motion picture brought a varied audience together, the person watching a movie was silent and solitary. In the same way, a drive in a car might open people to a new look at their surroundings. But sightseeing was not doing something active, like playing a sport.

Middle class and wealthy Americans of this era began to take vacations of a week or two. Some visited the new national parks, while others sought to improve their physical or moral well-being. Beach resorts reached out to large and varied groups of Americans. Atlantic City, New Jersey, had large numbers of visitors from all classes. The Florida vacation became part of American life. And for some, the transatlantic cruise to Europe was the height of social achievement.

Baseball

By the end of the late nineteenth century, baseball was already the national pastime. It was played by children and adults. Unlike football, it did not require much special gear, just a baseball, bat, and glove. Neighborhood parks built during this era had baseball diamonds for amateurs.

Professional baseball also grew in popularity. The annual audience for professional baseball grew dramatically. In 1900, it was about 3.4 million people. In 1910, it doubled, to about 6.8 million, and by the end of the 1910s, it was 9.3 million. Several elements helped to spur its growth. For one, there were more teams to follow. In 1900, there was one major league, the National League, and 13 minor leagues. The American League was founded in 1901, and two years later, the first World Series was played between the leagues' top teams. In 1909, President William Howard Taft began the tradition of throwing out the first ball. This sealed baseball's reputation as the national pastime. By 1912, there were 33 minor leagues.

Professional baseball appealed to men, women, and children. Seats varied in price, depending on location, so people of all classes could attend. Until radio became popular in the 1920s, Americans followed teams in the sports pages of daily newspapers. There, sportswriters like the *Atlanta Journal*'s Grantland Rice recreated the games' drama and promoted baseball as an ideal, all-American game.

Honus Wagner
(Library of Congress)

Top players during this era were the American League's Ty Cobb and Cy Young, and the National League's Honus Wagner. Cobb, who scored a record 2,245 runs, earned a reputation as one of the meanest players of all time. Yet when the Baseball Hall of Fame was established in 1936, he won the most votes of any player. Wagner, a shortstop nicknamed "the Flying Dutchman," was an all-around great player and became the fans' favorite partly for his cheerful, mannerly attitude. Young, baseball's first great pitcher, led the Boston Red Sox to win the first World Series over Wagner's Pittsburgh Pirates.

By 1915, the Red Sox had another pitcher who would reach even greater fame. George Herman "Babe" Ruth pitched nearly 30 scoreless innings in the 1918 World Series. But in 1920, Ruth was sold to the New York Yankees where he would become a symbol of the Roaring Twenties.

Over the decades, professional baseball generated a great deal of money. The game was a big business, and as the 1920s began, there was a scandal. In the 1919 World Series, there were rumors that some Chicago White Sox lost the series to collect gambling money. Eight players were put on trial. Seven were acquitted and charges were dropped on the eighth player. Yet they had broken the law, and the commissioner of baseball banned them from the game. One of them was star player "Shoeless Joe" Jackson. During the scandal, a young fan supposedly said to him, "Say it ain't so, Joe." He is said to have replied, "Yes kid, I'm afraid it is."

The "Black Sox Scandal" made the links between sports and gambling clear. But it did not erode people's interest in professional baseball. More huge professional stadiums were built across the country. Among them were the Polo Grounds in New York, Forbes Field in Pittsburgh, and Fenway Park in Boston.

Boxing, Football, and Driving

Before World War I began, boxing was as popular as baseball. Sports writers and social leaders approved of boxing as a healthful form of competition, and gyms were built for training.

Most professional fights were held in boxing rings, although some fights were held on private grounds. Major fights like those of heavyweight champion Jack Johnson made money in many ways. The spectators at ringside paid for seats. The people waiting in bars for fight reports paid for drinks between rounds. As with baseball, boxing news in the sports section also sold newspapers.

Other forms of boxing included bare-knuckle boxing, which was illegal in many states. It was practiced in clubs and private locations. Recreational fighting was also popular among some boys, and was considered a basic manhood skill.

Professional fighting became less popular as the century continued. It did not appeal to many social groups, the way baseball did. To many, it was a working man's game. But big-title fights still got a wide audience in the 1920s and beyond.

Football was a popular competitive sport on college campuses. In the 1900s and 1910s, teams from eastern and midwestern universities played to increasing crowds. The game was largely unregulated, and many injuries were caused by dangerous plays and tackles. In the 1910s, modifications like the forward pass and the line of scrimmage helped to make the game less dangerous and more easily understood by spectators. During the period, the game also became popular on smaller college campuses and schools.

Two leading football players of the era were were Knute Rockne of Notre Dame in Indiana and Jim Thorpe of Carlisle Indian School in Pennsylvania. A top student and reluctant athlete, Rockne helped change football from a ground game to one that combined passing and rushing. He went on to coach one of the best teams of all times at his Alma Mater. Thorpe, on the other hand, was an all-around athlete who played ten sports and won two Olympic Gold Medals. After his medals were stripped from him for playing baseball for money, Thorpe became the first big-name athlete to play football professionally, for the Canton (Ohio) Bulldogs. In 1920, he helped found the American Professional Football Association, which later became the National Football League.

The Indianapolis Speedway first opened in 1911.
(Library of Congress)

There was also driving, or "motoring" for sport. The long-distance automobile race, the Indianapolis 500, debuted in 1911. It was won by a driver who went at an average speed of 74 miles per hour. For the well-to-do, motoring was still a fad. Driving for fun involved wearing sporty clothes like a long coat called a duster and goggles. Sporty cars had special additions, like rumble seats. As the cost of the Model T came down by the mid-1920s, and working people bought them, the fad lessened and driving became a practical necessity.

Tennis, Cycling, and Rollerskating

In the 1910s, people of all ages played tennis and followed professional matches. While most players were members of country clubs and private schools, some of them made the game more appealing to the middle class. They did so by playing tennis in a more competitive and athletic way.

Before and after winning his first world championship in 1920, William "Big Bill" Tilden was especially influential. He was daring and creative in his play, and made each match seem like a battle and a drama. He made tennis more exciting to watch and to play.

Other sports had been more popular in the late nineteenth century, but were still played in the twentieth. Bicycling was still an adult activity. Thousands joined cycling clubs that sponsored social outings and races. As the price of bicycles dropped and their design made them safer, they were used by more children.

Rollerskating had become popular after the Civil War. By the twentieth century, it was a common childhood activity. Rollerskates were made of wood or metal and could be used on paved city streets. Adult skaters who wanted to skated at public skating rinks. Located in small towns and cities, the rinks charged admission to skate on highly polished wood floors. Skates could also be rented.

On the Stage

Serious (sometimes called legitimate) theater had a huge audience. The years between 1880 and 1920 were a golden era for theater. New York City was its center, and by 1904, 420 troupes toured the country. Most of the plays were melodramas that seem old-fashioned today, but one play, *Peter Pan*, remains popular. James Barrie wrote it in 1905 for Maude Adams, a beautiful actor from Utah who played the part of a boy who refuses to grow up. Actors of the period were among the nation's first celebrities, and they were important to a play's success. Ethel Barrymore had her first Broadway hit in 1901 and became a leading lady playing rich and charming young women. She and her brothers, John and Lionel, were part of a famous theater family.

A distinctly American form, the musical, gathered momentum early in the century. Among these works were Victor Herbert's operetta, *Babes in Toyland* in 1903, which introduced "March of the Toys." Other popular and prolific composers were Broadway musical writers Jerome Kern and George M. Cohan. Kern wrote tuneful songs for musical comedies that included *Very Good Eddie* (1915) and *Oh, Boy!* (1917). Cohan wrote, produced and acted in snappy musicals, including *Little Johnny Jones* (1904) and *Forty-five Minutes from Broadway* (1906). He was even better known for his patriotic songs, some from his musicals, some not. Among them were "Give My Regards to Broadway," "I'm a Yankee Doodle Dandy," and the World War I anthem, "Over There."

Also popular were Florenz Ziegfeld's annual Follies, where he showcased beautiful girls. Ziegfeld also introduced comedians Fanny Brice, Eddie Cantor and Will Rogers, and Bert Williams, Broadway's first African American star.

Vaudeville was even more popular. The on-stage variety show appealed to working- and middle-class patrons. In an average show, there might be song-and-dance pairs, physical comedy acts, animal talent, and acrobats and jugglers. Acts traveled on circuits, or systems, across the country. Special shows for children and families kept out racy acts. At the turn of the century, vaudeville houses had added motion pictures as an extra attraction. Movies, then, were about a minute long. By 1900, a one-reel motion picture ran about ten minutes, the length of a vaudeville act. It fit nicely into the program.

A turn-of-the-twentieth-century poster promotes The Great Gotham Stock Company, a New York City theatrical troupe. (Library of Congress)

Motion Pictures

At first, movies were bunched together and shown frequently at houses called nickelodeons. Befitting the name, the cost was

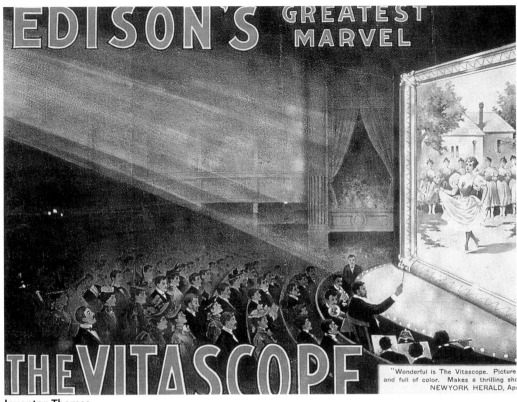

"Wonderful is The Vitascope. Picture and full of color. Makes a thrilling sho
NEW YORK HERALD, Apr

Inventor Thomas Edison first created the Vitascope in 1896. His invention opened the way for the start of the movie industry.
(Library of Congress)

five cents. The low price and the simple subjects made early movies appeal mainly to non-English speaking, working-class audiences. Usually they told a simple story like Edwin S. Porter's *The Great Train Robbery* (1903), about a hold-up and a chase. These movies did not appeal to the middle or upper class.

Soon multi-reel features were shown in fancier movie houses that seemed more respectable for families and the middle class. By 1910, about 10 million people went to the movies, a number that increased greatly each year of the decade. As with literature, popular subjects were Bible stories, Westerns, adventures, and dramas. Series of movies that told a story in installments became popular. Among them was *The Perils of Pauline*, about a plucky, trouble-prone young woman. Westerns with William S. Hart and slapstick comedies with Mack Sennett's Keystone Kops and Charlie Chaplin were popular. Dramas based on Bible stories were usually serious and expensive.

In 1915, the success of D.W. Griffiths's movie *The Birth of a Nation* established the feature film as a popular art form for a wide audience. Moviegoers paid a record high price to see the nearly three-hour movie about the Civil War and Reconstruction.

However, the movie caused great protests from African Americans and others who called it racist because of its positive portrayal of the Ku Klux Klan.

By 1920, many vaudeville houses were being converted to movie palaces. Technology was changing entertainment. Instead of looking at live players on stage, people watched shadows flickering on a screen. When actors began to speak aloud in 1927, the transformation would be complete.

Music

American music was developing a distinctive national sound. Composers drew from both European and African American traditions. Lyrics contained shared American sentiments and emotions that would reach a wide audience. The center of this new music was known as Tin Pan Alley, and it had many outlets. It could be found in stage shows, sheet music, and phonograph records.

Even though the radio would not become popular until the 1920s, people had many venues to hear new music. Some attended musical theater on Broadway and at local show houses. They might purchase sheet music and play the latest songs on the piano that was standard in middle- and upper-class homes.

Others paid to hear recordings on a public phonograph that was in a store or soda fountain. The cost was five cents per song. More and more, people listened to their own phonographs. In the mid-1910s, over half a million machines were sold each year. Most were four-foot tall handsome pieces of furniture. By 1920, many of these machines had replaced the family piano in the parlor. Rather than play themselves, people listened to a machine that reproduced musical sounds.

Newspapers and Magazines

Even though movies and the phonograph competed for attention, Americans continued to read in wide variety. Nearly everyone got the news from a newspaper, whether daily or weekly.

Especially important was the urban daily newspaper, which was growing in number and readers. In 1900, there were over 2,200 metropolitan, or city, newspapers, and about 15 million people bought them daily. A city had several different newspapers, each representing a different political slant and writing style. For example, New York City newspapers included the *Journal*, the *Times*, the *Tribune*, and the *World*, among others. These papers had many printings during the day and printed special editions for an important news story, like the 1911 Triangle Shirtwaist Fire. Despite the many printings, the papers were either morning or evening newspapers. Morning papers appealed to the reader riding to work in the morning or who wanted to catch up on the previous day's baseball scores, while evening papers appealed to workers ending a shift in the late afternoon. Recent additions to daily newspapers also made people want to buy the paper every day. Among them were the big Sunday paper, the daily columnist, and the comics. By the 1910s, millions of Americans bought the paper for the women's page, or Finley Peter Dunne's columns about "Mr. Dooley's" Chicago, or the "Yellow Kid" comics.

Rural papers also had great importance. Usually written and published by one person, they were the voice for a town or county. About 18 million people bought some rural weekly. In areas that did not get city newspapers, it was the main source of news.

Weekly and monthly magazines were standard additions to twentieth-century reading. They informed readers who wanted to keep up with changing politics, business, and styles. Improved printing techniques and lower mailing rates made magazines cheaper and more attractive.

General interest magazines aimed at the family were among the most popular. By the 1910s, the *Saturday Evening Post* was the leading general interest magazine, with a circulation of two million readers. In addition to profiling business leaders and printing literature by current writers like Theodore Dreiser, the *Post* gave political commentary. It had conservative Republican ideas, which matched many of the magazine's readers. In its words and cover illustrations by Norman Rockwell, it painted an idealized picture of American life. Its competition was *Collier's*, another general interest magazine.

Women's magazines such as the *Ladies' Home Journal* and *McCall's* presented modern decorating styles and comforting ideas about everyday morals. Other magazines appealed to special interests, such as health and literature. The flashy *Frank Leslie's Illustrated Newspaper* was a combination newspaper and magazine. It had detailed reports of crimes and low characters and was widely available in men's meeting places like barber shops. Magazines would become even more popular in the 1920s, with the debuts of *Time*, *Reader's Digest*, and *The New Yorker*.

Books

Reading books was a common activity for turn-of-the-century families. Some families had their own libraries. Others patronized the local public library. They read in the parlor, on the porch, or at the bedside. For children, there were books written especially for them. Youth literature had become popular in the late nineteenth century. Among the most popular were the hundreds of titles in action-filled Nancy Drew and Hardy Boys series. The books taught resourcefulness and clean living while also telling an exciting story. (Comic books would not come along until 1929.)

The Virginian, by Owen Wister, was one of the top-selling books of its time. (Library of Congress)

Much popular adult fiction appealed to women. Much of it was nostalgic, rural, and fanciful, like *Rebecca of Sunnybrook Farm* by Kate Douglas Wiggin. Novels about the West also became popular after the success of Owen Wister's *The Virginian* and the novels of Zane Grey.

Other authors of the period were more ambitious. Theodore Dreiser's *Sister Carrie* in 1900 shocked people with its depiction of a young woman who goes to the city and becomes supported by a man who is not her husband. Edith Wharton examined social class in America in her 1905 *House of Mirth*. Willa Cather's spare prose in her frontier story *O Pioneers!* in 1913 foretold a style that would become more popular later in the century.

Public Parks

For those who found home stifling, there was the public park. Many large cities began to build parks during the nineteenth century, and more were built during the early twentieth century. Cities like New York, Chicago, and Boston had dozens of neighborhood parks. Their playgrounds and simple walkways offered a safe place for children to play and a vision of the country in the crowded city. Reflecting a new concern for physical fitness, the neighborhood park often had a baseball field or swimming pool.

Like other ideas for public improvement, the neighborhood park was promoted by urban social reformers. Chicago's Hull

**New York City's
Coney Island.**
(Library of Congress)

House founder Jane Addams and New York housing reformer Jacob Riis worked to have playgrounds built across the country. They helped to found the Playground Association of America in 1906.

Larger parks, like New York's Central Park, were hundreds of acres and had elaborate gardens and walkways. They also had areas for formal public entertainment, like bandshells and amphitheaters. Often created by leading architects, these large parks were designed to beautify the city and show the city's importance.

Amusement Parks

While public parks emphasized nature, amusement parks offered an escape into fantasy. They were also supposed to remind people of rural county fairs from their childhood and resort cities like Atlantic City. Run by private companies, they were not meant to improve society or make a city look good. They aimed to entertain.

Most big cities had at least one amusement center. As it had been for years, the best-known was New York's Coney Island. It had exciting rides such as roller coasters and fantastic mechanical creations like the ride called "A Trip to the Moon." A walkway or boardwalk surrounded the rides and offered stage shows, restaurants, and snacks such as cotton candy and peanuts.

Amusement centers also offered plenty of people-watching. People from all classes went to the amusement park. Like other new forms of twentieth-century entertainment, it brought people together in a communal American experience.

Social Clubs and Fraternal Organizations

In their spare time, many Americans formed social ties in specialized organizations. Fraternal organizations such as the mostly Protestant Masons had claimed early presidents as their members. Other groups began to gain importance in the late nineteenth century, as immigration brought more religions and ethnic backgrounds into the nation. Among them were groups such as the Ancient Order of Hibernians (Irish), the Prudent Patricians of Pompeii (Italian), and the Viking Council of the Mystic Brotherhood (Scandanavian).

Other groups were for members of a religion, as the Knights of Columbus was for Roman Catholics. Still other groups promoted farm and rural interests (the Grange) or business interests (Lions and Rotarians). They were open to a wider membership, and were supposed to show a town's unity and strength. All the groups had regular meetings and community-wide programs, such as Fourth of July picnics or St. Patrick's Day parades. Many men's groups had associations for wives, but women, too, formed their own. The Daughters of the American Revolution, whose members claimed an ancestor from that war, became prominent in this era.

For boys and girls, scouting came to the United States from Britain. Boy Scouts were incorporated in the United States in 1910 by Chicagoan William Boyce. They numbered 300,000 by 1919. In Savannah, Georgia, Juliette Gordon Low founded the Girl Scouts in 1912.

Vacations

While many workers took an afternoon break at amusement parks, others took days-long vacations. Among middle-class workers, one- to two-week vacations were standard. Generally, businesses gave paid vacation time to the office or professional staff. Laborers or per-hour workers rarely got paid vacation time.

Like other leisurely pursuits in the early century, vacations were often ways to improve oneself. There were many choices. For nature lovers, there were trips to U.S. national parks. By the mid-1910s, national parks included Grand Canyon, Yellowstone, and Yosemite. People traveled by train or car and stayed in a hotel or campground. To improve health, there were trips to mountainous areas like Colorado. The high altitude and clean air were said to improve lung conditions like tuberculosis. To improve muscle and joint conditions, people went to areas known for healthful waters, like Saratoga Springs, New York. For spiritual improve-

The *Titanic*

For years, transatlantic travel had been popular with members of high society. Well-heeled passengers took cruises for social and business reasons.

In 1912, the new luxury ocean liner *Titanic* was the height of modern technology and high style. The ship had fine restaurants, ballrooms, and golf ranges. There were modern bathrooms, and tailors and valets to take care of personal needs.

On April 10, the *Titanic* made its maiden, or first, voyage. To protect its passengers, the nearly 50,000-ton vessel had compartments and doors that were watertight. Those were believed to protect the ship and keep it from sinking. If there were problems, the ship had 16 lifeboats and four backup lifeboats. They could take on about 1,200 passengers.

But the ship was much larger and carried more than 2,200 passengers and crew.

On April 13, the *Titanic* hit a huge iceberg at 11:40 p.m. When the crew saw the ship was sinking, it brought women and children to the lifeboats. Between midnight and about 2 a.m., all the lifeboats were launched. Mostly they contained first- and second-class women and children. But the boats were not full. Some people still thought the boat could not sink and did not want to ride in a cold, tiny lifeboat. Most steerage passengers were not offered places in lifeboats, even if there was room.

When the *Titanic* hit the iceberg, the crew sent radio distress signals to ships in the area. According to one wireless operator, the message read, "S.S. *Titanic* ran into iceberg. Sinking fast." But most of the calls for help were not answered, and some 1,500 people died in the waters. Among them were American industrialist John Jacob Astor and the ship's crew of 500. Only 705 people survived. Ninety-six percent of women and children in first-class survived, as did 89 percent of second-class women and children. But only 47 percent of women and children in lowest, steerage class were saved.

News about the *Titanic* sinking created an uproar in the United States. In addition to being upset at the death toll, many people were angry at how class determined which passengers were saved.

(Library of Congress)

ment, there were camps that offered a mix of physical exercise, and religious study. Protestants gathered at the Methodist-centered beach resort in Ocean Grove, New Jersey, or in Chatauqua, New York.

Still, many vacations had no serious purpose. They were ways to rest, show off, or experience the exotic. Some ethnic groups set up their own vacation areas. They were scenic regions such as the Catskill Mountain towns of New York that had hotels, cabins, and entertainment. Beautiful and expensive places like Mackinac Island, Michigan, and Cape May, New Jersey, were standard stops for the well-to-do and special trips for the middle class. Many Americans also felt it was important to travel abroad. Those who could afford it took ocean cruises across the Atlantic Ocean to Europe.

Two vacation areas showed the constant appeal of sun and surf. One was Florida. Towns along the Atlantic coast of Florida like Palm Beach were being developed, and handsome hotels were being built. In the twentieth century, people took the train or drove to Daytona Beach, St. Augustine, or other towns. They began the American tradition of the Florida vacation.

More well known and accessible at the time was Atlantic City, New Jersey. It was a popular vacation spot for all classes and ages, offering the Atlantic Ocean, boardwalks, and much people watching. After experiencing the big hotels, salt water taffy, and animal shows, a travel writer of the day said Atlantic City was a "dreadful place." And yet, he said, it was "exactly what the majority of us really like."

In the 1920s, Atlantic City grew even more gaudy. In 1921, it hosted its first Miss America pageant. Baseball remained popular, but other kinds of popular entertainment changed. Vaudeville declined, movies had sound, and the weekly newsmagazine started. Everything became faster, brighter, and louder.

Chapter Nine

Fashions and Fads

An early advertisement for women's clothing at Lord & Taylor department store (LEFT); **Three little boys dressed in "Little Lord Fauntleroy" outfits** (RIGHT). **Little Lord Fauntleroy was a character in a popular British novel from the 1890s.** (Library of Congress)

Many of the customs that began as fads and fashions in the early twentieth century are still with us today. People began to dress more comfortably than they had in the previous century. They aspired to buy their clothing at fancy new department stores. They began to eat healthier foods, such as salads made of lettuce and fruits like bananas, melon, and pineapple. They added new foods of questionable nutritional value like hot dogs, Jell-O, and carbonated drinks. And they began to chew gum and to eat in convenient self-service restaurants called automats. Unfortunately, it was during this period that smoking cigarettes became an all-American habit.

As suburbs developed, architectural styles became more varied. The elaborate mansions of the Victorian era progressed to an even more ornate Queen Anne style. But they had plenty of competition from a revival of colonial-inspired public buildings and new arts and craft–style homes with horizontal, clean lines. Indoors, people who could afford to created all white bathrooms that they cleaned and sanitized with a passion. Outdoors they tended their gardens and lawns.

For entertainment, adults played games like lawn tennis and ping-pong. They gathered in dance halls where they learned the latest dance steps. They took children to public and private amusement parks where they could enjoy merry-go-rounds and other pleasures.

Children had few toys, but some introduced during this period are still around. They include the teddy bear, Raggedy Ann dolls, and erector sets. Another toy, used mostly by adults, was the Ouija board. With its pointer under the players' fingers, it was supposed to spell out the future. Popular as it was, it never predicted the many changes that lay ahead.

Early Century Women's Fashions

At the beginning of the twentieth century, the Gibson Girl was the female ideal. Based on illustrations by Charles Dana Gibson, she was a tall, active young woman with floor-length dresses with high necks and long sleeves. Her long hair was swept into a bun. The hourglass defined the shape of a woman's body. Tight corsets with metal reinforcement made waists tiny and the upper and lower body oversized. They also made it difficult for women to breathe. Under their long skirts, women wore petticoats made of stiff fabric that rustled when they walked.

Well-to-do women had many clothes of a variety of fabrics—silk, wool, linen and cotton, often with lots of lace. Many of their clothes were made by private dressmakers because they were wealthy enough not to sew their own clothes, and mass-made clothing had not been perfected.

An upper-class woman changed her clothes many times each day to meet the needs of her social life. Almost always, she had help from her maid in buttoning or lacing her dresses or in arranging her hair in complicated styles. In the morning, she wore a dressing gown and wrapper, or robe. For afternoon social calls, she wore a walking suit. When she was young, it was made of light colors, and it grew darker as she aged. Her fancy boots were closed by buttons. A button hook was required to fasten them. For dinner, she wore a gown, or dining dress, of silk or some other dressy fabric. Its sleeves were puffy and large to accentuate her small waist. Satin slippers completed the outfit.

A middle-class woman had a much smaller wardrobe. By day, she wore a floor-length skirt and a high-necked blouse trimmed with lace. She might buy them in one of the fancy new department stores, and if she was fortunate, they were made in France. If she did not have a cook, she changed clothes to prepare dinner, then changed again into a different dress to dine.

A walking suit, for afternoon visiting.
(Dover Publications)

Working women had even smaller wardrobes. In business, they adapted the Gibson Girl look to include a long, dark skirt that could be worn several days at a time and a white blouse that could be changed every day. Teachers dressed in a similar style. If a woman worked in a factory, she had even fewer clothes and changed into a sleeping shift when she came home. Most working women had to sew their own clothing. Store-bought clothing, for them, was a luxury.

Nearly all women wore a hat and gloves. Hats were purchased from a milliner, or hatmaker. They were less elaborate than they had been in the late nineteenth century, but they still were decorated with flowers, fruit, and ribbons. Summer hats were made of straw. To demonstrate that it was unnecessary for them to work outdoors, well-to-do women took elaborate measures to protect themselves from the sun. Gloves were made of cotton, lace, or leather in different lengths, from the wrists to above the elbow. Some women carried a parasol. It looked like an umbrella, but it was only used in the sun. Often, it matched the woman's outfit.

Women's Fashion Changes

Gradually, women's clothing began to change during this period. As women entered the workforce, the old elaborate clothing was not practical. Manufactured clothing became more predictable. Sizes were becoming standard, and new chemical dyes created fabrics that did not fade. They were called fast colors because they set fast and remained true.

French designers had a big effect on American fashion. Before World War I, Paul Poiret introduced straight skirts, tunics, loose "harem" pants, and turbans inspired by workers' kerchiefs. Gabrielle (Coco) Chanel designed casual clothing known as sportswear. It was made of knitted fabrics. French designers put pockets onto women's clothing for the first time.

Other trends were influenced by celebrities. Dancer Irene Castle made headbands fashionable. Competitive swimmer Adeline Trapp wore a form-fitting short suit for a swim in 1909, and women began to abandon the long wool dresses they had worn into the water. Modern dancer Isadora Duncan and spy Mata Hari made long scarves and boas fashionable.

Dresses were made of lighter fabrics. One favorite was the white cotton "lingerie dress." Its lace inserts showed off a woman's bodice. Other women began to abandon high necked clothing, especially in the evening. Clergymen complained that lower necklines revealed lower moral standards, and physicians worried that they would lead to illness.

As women adopted the French fashion of dresses that hung straight from the shoulders, they abandoned their many petticoats. Instead they wore cotton or silk pantaloons—slips shaped like trousers that allowed them to dance more freely. The French-designed brassiere was introduced but would not be popular until elastic was added in the 1920s.

Finally, the corset was tossed out in the mid-1910s. Clothing reformers and health officials were delighted. During World War I, American women demonstrated their dislike of corsets and their patriotism when they donated their corsets to the war effort. The 28,000 tons of steel in them built two battleships.

Illustrator Maxfield Parrish created the new image of fashion. The young, not-yet-fully-developed woman was the ideal. For books and magazines, Parrish drew figures that were more adolescent than adult, more boyish than womanly. The scene was set for the flappers of the 1920s.

Men's Fashions

Men's fashions also reflected their place in society and the work they did. A well-to-do man had many suits, usually made by a tailor. Each came with an extra pair of trousers and a waistcoat, or vest. His ties were made of silk, and sometimes his shirts were too. He wore European-styled jackets like the knee-length frock coat, which might be single- or double-breasted. Dress wear was a cutaway jacket whose long back tails tapered from the waist at the front. He also had a more casual short "sack suit" jacket, which he might wear with a colorful shirt by Arrow, an American manufacturer. The Arrow Shirt Man was becoming the male model.

Well-dressed men typically had three overcoats: a raincoat, an automobile coat, and a short overcoat. In cool weather they wore homburg hats with high crowns and rolled brims, or other felt hats. In the summer, they wore flat-brimmed straw boaters. Their hands were gloved.

Standard clothing sizes for men's clothes were developed during the Civil War, and ready-made suits were available now. They

Men's fashions, as advertised in the Sears, Roebuck catalog for 1900.
(Library of Congress)

were made of wool, serge, hopsack, and for the summer, seersucker. Middle-class professionals and office workers might buy these suits, which were often made of less expensive fabrics than those made by a tailor. Cotton shirts had no collars. A fresh collar of stiff fabric was attached every day. Middle-class men usually owned no formal wear, but they may have had a leisure outfit like a baseball uniform or a casual jacket.

Police had worn dark blue uniforms with badges since the late nineteenth century. Now other public workers like subwaymen and mail carriers wore uniforms too. Uniforms promoted solidarity and a serious attitude toward work. They also made it unnecessary for workers to provide their own clothes. Factory workers wore collarless shirts and work pants of coarse fabric.

Working-class men wore caps rather than hats. They were made of heavy fabrics with a half-brim to protect them from the sun or wind. They might own one suit, often left over from their wedding. They wore it to funerals, religious services, and other people's weddings.

No matter what class, men began the century with facial hair. Well-to-do and middle-class men tended to wear sideburns and, sometimes, beards. Immigrant working-class men were more likely to wear mustaches like those worn in Europe.

Men's Fashion Change, Too

As the century wore on, special clothing for safaris, tennis, and motoring gained acceptance in the upper classes. The sack suit changed into formal wear as the tuxedo. Since modern men spent more time indoors, they could swap their long wool underwear for cotton sleeveless, knee-length underwear called union suits, or BVDs, after their manufacturer.

Wrist watches were introduced by French designer Cartier in 1904. Accustomed to pocket watches with long chains, many men regarded them as effeminate. But trendsetters like dancer Vernon Castle helped to make them popular. Eventually, ready-made suits were made without watch pockets, and the wristwatch became the twentieth-century timepiece.

During World War I, safety razors were given to soldiers. They made shaving easier and more popular. After the war, sideburns, beards, and mustaches gave way to clean-shaven faces.

What Children Wore

Before the 1920s when psychologists began to divide childhood into stages of development, there were no special clothes designs for toddlers, young children, pre-teens and teenagers. Babies were dressed in cotton gowns that allowed easy movement.

Well-to-do and middle-class little boys were dressed like girls until they were six. They wore dresses and their hair was long. Then they were put into knickers, or baggy knee-length trousers, for play every day. For portraits or a special occasion, boys might be dressed in a short, fancy velvet suit inspired by the 1886 British novel, *Little Lord Fauntleroy*. The Man O' War suit came with a sailor shirt and long trousers. Otherwise, boys wore short dress pants until they reached adulthood. Like their fathers', their dress shirts were collarless. Special collars might be attached.

Working-class boys followed the same patterns, but their clothes were hand-me-downs or homemade from other family members' clothes or from fabric sacks that held flour.

Girls wore dresses for every occasion: school, play, and special events. Upper-class girls had more and fancier dresses. Middle-class girls' dresses might be made at home from high-fashion patterns. Dressy clothes were made of silk or velvet and trimmed with lace. They wore bows in their hair and dress boots like their mothers', with tiny buttons.

For play, these girls wore middy dresses, whose collars were square in the back and came to a V in the front or round-necked blouson dresses with dropped waists that made movement easy. Usually the dress was covered by a long apron, or pinafore. It was white and could be washed more frequently than the dress. Black cotton or wool stockings were worn year-round with lace-up boots.

Working-class girls wore dresses of cheaper fabric and without adornment. Some straight dresses, called shifts, were popular. They wore the same dresses for school and play, and they might have a special dress for religious services and special occasions.

When girls entered puberty, they learned to put their hair up with hairpins in a bun. They wore long dresses that hid their legs, and for part of the early century, they also wore a corset. Someone had to lace it up for them. Then they had to relearn how to sit and stand in it.

Girls stopped wearing corsets in the 1910s when it went out of fashion for adult women. Now teen-aged girls became the fashion idea. No longer did they have to try to look more mature than they were. Suddenly, adult women wanted to look like them.

Toy Fads

Toy manufacturing was a small part of the U.S. economy. It accounted for less than $12 million in 1912. Yet some toys were so popular that they became fads. Among them were cast-iron mechanical toys like cars, airplanes and war vehicles. There were also miniature sewing machines and novelty banks. The erector set debuted in 1913. With it boys could construct metal buildings and machinery that moved with batteries.

Mass-manufactured dolls became popular, too. The teddy bear, named for President Theodore Roosevelt, was the most popular. It was inspired by a story that the president had refused to kill a bear cub on a hunting trip. The plastic Kewpie Doll with its brightly painted face was first produced in 1911. Red-haired Raggedy Ann became a sensation in 1918. She had yarn hair, button eyes, and a triangle-shaped nose. Both dolls came with stories about them. They were early examples of product tie-ins.

Both boys and girls liked to draw with Crayola crayons. They were introduced in 1903. The sled served the popular ideas of the day that children needed an active, outdoor life and exercise. The Flexible Flyer was the best-known brand.

The leading board game was not primarily for children. It was the fortune-telling Ouija board. (The name was made of the French and German words for "yes.") Players moved the fortune-telling piece along the board until it stopped at an answer. The game sold over one million sets in 1918 alone.

Amusements

Many of the sports that later became more serious began as faddish social activities. One was lawn tennis, a game played by stylishly dressed upper-class women who talked as much as they played. Ping-pong was a popular family game and often played on the dining table. When played in mixed doubles with males and females, it could be quite intense.

In the many public and amusement parks were merry-go-rounds or carousels. Children circled on wooden horses as they tried to catch a brass ring suspended with an arm's reach. The rider who grabbed it won a prize—or a free ride.

Dancing became more intimate and informal, like many other aspects of life. The last century's waltzes had kept couples upright and separated. The fox trot, turkey trot, bunny hug, and especially, the tango, brought their bodies close together. Some cities even banned the tango.

New dance halls were places where respectable people could go to learn the latest dance. Young people gathered to socialize and practice the latest steps. Celebrity choreographers Vernon and Irene Castle introduced many of these dances. People might practice them at home to a phonograph recording or a piano played to the latest sheet music. As they did with other celebrities, some Americans imitated the Castles' fashions. When Irene Castle cut her hair short before she went to the hospital for an operation,

Vernon and Irene Castle (Library of Congress)

Meet Me at the Fair

The Louisiana Purchase Exposition of 1904 in St. Louis, Missouri, marked the 100th anniversary of the 1803 Louisiana Purchase. The 20 million people who visited it called it the 1904 World's Fair. For most, it was a grand entertainment. There was so much anticipation of the event that it had its own song, "Meet Me In St. Louis," by Kerry Mills and Andrew B. Sterling.

Many examples of the latest American technology were on display. Buildings were lit with thousands of electric lights. There were 100 different cars at the automobile exhibit. For a bird's-eye view of the fair, there was the world's largest Ferris wheel. It had been brought from the 1893 Chicago Midway.

The fair had its own curiosities. There was the all-butter sculpture of President Roosevelt and a bear statue made of prunes. On the midway were several foods that later became some of America's favorites. They included iced tea, sliced bread, and ice cream cones.

short hair became popular. It paved the way for bobbed hair of the 1920s.

Food Fads

In this era, Americans made their diets more balanced by eating a lighter breakfast, less meat, and more fruit. Between meals, they had many food crazes.

The move to eat more healthfully came partly from the influence of French cooking. Green salads became an accepted course, and the lettuce to make them became the latest fashion. It was called iceberg lettuce. It was also known as "head lettuce" because its leaves were packed close together in a round shape. Americans had not seen such hardy lettuce. It could be shipped cross-country on trains and it was still crisp in the salad bowl. Iceberg remained the standard lettuce for salad for decades to come.

Fruits new to the American diet also became fads. Among them were honeydew melon, bananas, grapefruit, and pineapple. Pineapple was put into cans and shipped to grocers across the country. It was eaten plain or put into new desserts like pineapple upside-down cake. Grapefruit growers worked to make their fruit sweeter-tasting, and it became part of a healthy breakfast.

The five-cent sausage in a roll called the hot dog became popular at New York's Coney Island amusement park. Hot dogs soon were sold at food stands across the nation.

When the chopped beef sandwich known as the hamburger was introduced in Connecticut in 1900, the century's most popular casual foods were in place.

Carbonated beverages such as Coca-Cola and Dr Pepper had been introduced late in the last century. They were created by pharmacists mostly as a sort of tonic to give drinkers a lift. The coca leaf left traces of cocaine in the early drinks. By the twentieth century, the strongest drug in them was caffeine mixed with large amounts of sugar. These beverages were joined by Pepsi Cola (to treat dyspepsia, or indigestion), Royal Crown Cola and A&W root beer. Eventually, the health pretenses of these drinks were dropped, but they remained popular.

As servants became less common in America's kitchens, quick and easy foods gained popularity. That is how a powdered mix of gelatin, sugar, and fruit flavor became a very popular American dessert, with the help of a little advertising. Introduced by New York medicine manufacturer Pearl Wait and named by his wife, Jell-O was sold to the Genessee Pure Food Company at the beginning of the century. Jell-O could be mixed by hand and chilled in the icebox or on a window ledge in cold weather. Then there came the Jell-O Girl, Elizabeth King. Often appearing with Kewpie Dolls, King gave Jell-O the image of freshness and youth. Salesmen gave away dessert spoons and recipe books. Everyone wanted Jell-O.

Architectural Fashions

In the nineteenth century, wealthy people had built mansions with many rooms, fancy decorations, broad porches and tall, gabled roofs. Some continued to do so. The Queen Anne style outdid itself by adding even more ornaments to the older Victorian style.

A promotional calendar for Coca-Cola. (Courtesy of the Coca-Cola Company)

At the same time, other builders looked to early American history for their inspiration. Initiated by architects McKim, Mead and White, the Colonial Revival style was patterned on the Georgian and Federal buildings of New England. Usually built of red brick, these buildings often had porches, or porticos, supported by white columns. The style was popular for banks, schools and churches, but new suburbanites sometimes chose it for their homes. No matter what the purpose, Colonial Revival buildings were usually much larger than the originals.

Another movement, which began as rebellion against industrialization, had come from Europe. The Arts and Craft style emphasized clean, horizontal lines and the work of skilled craftsmen. Architect Frank Lloyd Wright developed a truly American vision of this style in his Prairie homes. A Midwesterner, Wright first built Prairie homes in Chicago's Oak Park and River Forest suburbs.

The houses featured roofs with broad, low eaves that projected away from the house, casement windows that opened outward rather than up and down, and large, low chimneys with hearths that he considered the home's center. In time, these homes were in demand by wealthy people across the Midwest. In California, the Arts and Craft movement found its expression through architect brothers Charles and Henry Greene. The Greenes were additionally influenced by Japanese model homes they saw at the Chicago Exposition (see feature on page 134). They took the simple bungalow style, which originated in India, and turned it into modern, flowing homes for the rich. Skilled in woodworking and metal working, they carefully designed every element.

People with middle class budgets might turn to more modest bungalows with plans introduced by Gustav Stickley through his magazine *The Craftsman*, introduced in 1904. Stickley sought to "employ only those forms and materials which make for simplicity, individuality, and dignity of effect." He also designed furniture with simple lines for his houses, as Wright and the Greenes did, too. Homebuilders on an even tighter budget might turn to Sears, Roebuck or Montgomery Ward for a kit of plans and materials. Simple bungalows became a popular home style for families with no servants. They were often first houses for people who moved away from city apartments.

Outside, Americans tended their lawns, if they had them. Gardening had been popular since the late nineteenth century. While the middle and working classes grew vegetables and some flowers, the upper-class created gardens of ornamental plants. Now, a more natural garden and a lawn was the ideal. Community groups like the Rotary Club had contests for the greenest lawn with the fewest weeds. The perfect lawn was supposed to be a ticket to social success.

More Change Ahead

As the economy moved from agriculture to industry and the population from rural to urban, more Americans than ever were poised for prosperity. Though they could not imagine it, the pace of change would become more rapid. Transportation and communications would continue to improve. Americans had cast off many of the fashions and habits that inhibited them. They would cast off even more.

Bibliography

Bowen, Ezra, ed. *This Fabulous Century: Vol I 1900–1910*. New York: Time-Life Books, 1991.

_____. *This Fabulous Century: Vol II 1910–1920*. New York: Time-Life Books, 1991.

Cooper, John Milton. *Pivotal Decades: The United States, 1900-1920*. New York: W.W. Norton & Company, 1990.

Furnas, J.C. *The Americans: A Social History of the United States, 1587-1914*. New York: G.P. Putnam's Sons, 1969.

Green, Harvey. *The Uncertainty of Everyday Life, 1915-1945*. New York: HarperCollins Publishers, Inc., 1992.

Groner, Alex. *The History of American Business and Industry*. New York: American Heritage, 1972.

Lord, Walter. *The Good Years: From 1900 to the First World War*. New York: Harper & Brothers, Publishers, 1960.

Schlereth, Thomas J. *Victorian America: Transformations in Everyday Life, 1876-1915*. New York: HarperPerennial, 1991.

Schnurnberger, Lynn. *Let There Be Clothes: 40,000 Years of Fashion*. New York: Workman Publishing, 1991.

Sullivan, Mark. *Our Times: America at the Birth of the Twentieth Century*. New York: Scribner, 1926, 1996.

Index

Note: Page numbers in *italics* refer to illustrations.